IMPACT and
INfLUENCE

To my boys
– two very special people

RICHARD HALE and PETER WHITLAM

IMPACT and CT
INFLUENCE

tools and techniques for
creating a lasting impression

KOGAN
PAGE

First published in 1999

Kogan Page Limited
120 Pentonville Road
London
N1 9JN
UK

Kogan Page Limited
163 Central Avenue, Suite 4
Dover
NH 03820
USA

British Library Cataloguing in Publication Data

A CIP record for this book is available from the British Library.

ISBN 0 7494 3084 2

Typeset by Saxon Graphics Ltd, Derby
Printed and bound by Clays Ltd, St Ives plc

CONTENTS

PREFACE

In times of rapid change and uncertainty, when organizational structures are shifting and changing constantly, there are fewer and fewer opportunities to influence others by the use of traditional power and authority. Instead individuals increasingly have to rely on their personal impact and their influencing skills. This book recognizes the evolving dynamic and aims to enhance your abilities in the critical area.

Some have said that these skills are innate and, as such, difficult to learn. We contest this view and make a continuing contribution to the subject by building on our previously acclaimed work. We show, for example, how, through effective planning and preparation, it is possible to considerably improve the impact that you make on others and hence improve your influencing abilities.

This book is unique in that it links previously published influencing skills research with practical experiences gained whilst developing the influencing skills of others in both group and one-to-one settings. The authors, in short, build on their previous successful work, providing new insights as well as additional tools and techniques.

BACKGROUND

In 1996 we wrote the much acclaimed *The Power of Personal Influence* which was born out of two aspects of our work with international managers. The book's success and the subsequent demand for training in the sphere of impact and influencing skills have driven us to update our research: this new book represents the output of that process.

Whilst our training is focused primarily on the context of individuals in organizations, inevitably we pursue the subject of influencing in everyday situations. Arguably most human encounters provide opportunities for influencing other people. We believe strongly that the skills we address are transferable from one context to another. In a similar way we believe that the international nature of our research tends to suggest that many of our findings hold good across a range of cultures. Indeed, throughout the book references are made to the challenge of influencing across cultures and to research findings about cultural norms.

HOW TO GET THE MOST FROM THE **BOOK**

This book is focused specifically at individuals who are concerned with improving the impression they make on others, the impact they have and the influencing skills that they employ.

It is written in a very practical and user-friendly format. Experience suggests that learning is more powerful if you are able to interact with the content. To that end you are encouraged at various stages in this book to think of real influencing situations that you find yourself in and to reflect on them using the questions we pose. You are encouraged to link them to the ideas contained in the book in order to develop your own conclusions, thus enabling you to plan what you are going to do differently next time. Indeed, to help you bring the ideas to life we provide a whole chapter full of practical ideas that will help you enhance your influencing skills.

This approach to learning, an approach which permeates all our work, stems from the ideas of Kolb (1984), which suggest that we learn through a process of experiencing (doing something), reflecting (considering what has been done), theorizing (coming to conclusions) and finally planning (deciding what needs to be done in order to improve). We encourage you to relate the content of this book to your own experiences and through this process identify actions you can take in order to enhance your effectiveness in the areas of impressions, impact and influence. We also move you beyond the skills dimension of influencing to the mental processes that underpin effective influencing and as a result give you a comprehensive and up-to-date text on the subject of influencing in today's multicultural world. In order to support your development in impact, impressions and influence we provide case studies, called storyboards, based on real situations and people.

UNDERSTANDING OUR **APPROACH**

Our approach to influencing is very much an analytical and systematic one. The specific competences that need to be practised in order to influence effectively are identified, defined and discussed. This competence approach gives you access to the whole influencing picture through its component parts, making the subject manageable and allowing you to focus on what you need to do to develop effective influencing skills. As a discipline this approach will also help you to identify the specific strengths and weaknesses in others, as well as in yourself, providing an additional opportunity for learning. We do not, however, confine ourselves to simple skill acquisition but also provide information and ideas on the cognitive processes that will allow you to develop your influencing abilities.

STRUCTURE AND STYLE OF THE **BOOK**

The book consists of nine integrated chapters following the authors' newly revised systematic model of influencing. This preface provides the background to understanding the book and its key concepts. Each chapter thereafter follows the same structure, with stated objectives, development of ideas and pause for thought questions. The development of ideas represents the content of each chapter. Ideas are presented and explored using a number of models, techniques and concepts, and are drawn from our experiences of working with organizations such as Allied Domecq, Coca-Cola, 3M, BP, Esselte, Lotus Software Corporation, Motorola and Nestlé, as well as from up-to-date literature.

In order to enhance ease of access, we now provide a summary of each chapter.

CHAPTER 1: UNDERSTANDING INFLUENCE

This chapter commences by seeking to define influence. We consider the common barriers to effective influence, including psychological resistance, failing to manage the hierarchy of change, ineffective listening and lack of commitment. Each barrier is then considered and solutions sought.

The chapter moves on to provide the reader with a six-stage model, the Model of Successful Influencing, which is outlined in Figure 0.1.

The initial chapter goes on to suggest that each stage of the model requires or highlights certain competences, although we are not suggesting a definitive linkage between a stage of the model and a competence. For example, rapport building is a key competence in the pleasantries stage of influencing; however, the ability to develop rapport is still a requirement at the exploring possibilities stage of the process.

The stages and the competences associated with each stage are explored and discussed in the subsequent chapters as outlined below.

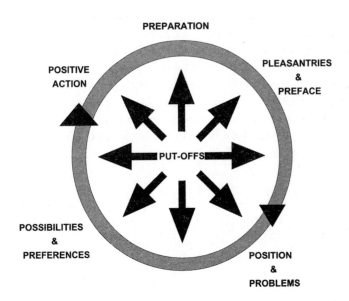

Figure 0.1 The Model of Successful Influencing

Chapter 2: Preparation: information gathering

The competence covered is information gathering. The chapter commences by recognizing that planning and information gathering are key in influencing and we explore what is meant by planning. We introduce you to the issue of influencing styles and how to prepare to influence individuals with differing styles. We discuss values and why it is important to understand someone's values before attempting to influence; and lastly we highlight the need to understand cultural differences when preparing to influence.

Chapter 3: Preparation: mental readiness

The competence covered is mental readiness. This chapter further explores the subject of planning and preparation by discussing the importance of mental readiness. It describes the way some individuals are beaten before they start to influence, mainly because of inappropriate personal attitudes and beliefs. The chapter asks you to consider your own beliefs in order to help you enhance your effectiveness as an influencer.

CHAPTER 4: PLEASANTRIES AND PREFACE

In this chapter, the book focuses on pleasantries and the associated competences of impact and rapport building. The chapter considers a number of ways in which impact can be developed and includes reference to the importance of impressions management. We go on to suggest that many people fail to create positive impact and explore the most common reason that this occurs. Next we probe the most effective way of building rapport or developing relationships with others and we discuss models that illustrate how effective relationships develop.

This chapter also focuses on preface, the gaining of the other person's attention. The competence explored is gaining and maintaining levels of attention. At the most fundamental level it is about gaining interest from the uninterested. Words and behaviours can gain attention; here we discuss the opportunities for using both approaches.

CHAPTER 5: POSITION AND PROBLEMS

The key skill at the position stage is understanding. Position is seen as the foundation block on which the influencing process is based. Without effective understanding of the current position, and the subsequent identification of the inherent problems, it is unlikely that effective influence will take place.

The problems stage is primarily concerned with identifying and defining the problems associated with the current position. The reader is provided with problem-solving models. The key skills at this stage are listening and questioning. These are explored and special reference is made to the skill of three-level questioning, a technique designed to allow the values and beliefs of the other person to be identified. Once such values have been identified, it is increasingly easy to influence the other person and to appeal to their values. We describe how both parties need to develop a joint vision as a conclusion to this stage of the influencing process.

CHAPTER 6: POSSIBILITIES, PREFERENCES AND POSITIVE ACTION

This chapter focuses primarily on the competences of verbal persuasiveness and building credibility. The reader is provided with a wide range of persuasive techniques. Credibility is concerned with raising esteem. It is about preparing the other person to accept our ideas by making them more secure and trustful. Techniques like slowly increasing credibility are discussed.

Positive action is the final stage of the Model of Successful Influencing, and is concerned primarily with tenacity. It is recognized that asking for commitment to positive action, or as a salesman would describe it, 'asking for the order', is a difficult step to undertake.

CHAPTER 7: NON-VERBAL COMMUNICATION

Here we deviate from the Model of Successful Influencing and explore the subject of non-verbal communication, which accounts for the majority of communication, as a chapter in its own right. We explore the key competence of reading and using body language.

CHAPTER 8: DEALING WITH PUT-OFFS

In this chapter the critical skill is assertion. For many individuals this chapter presents the greatest challenge, being about dealing with the objections of the other person. As suggested earlier, the skills we describe as the component parts of influencing do not relate exclusively to single stages in the Model of Successful Influencing. This is very evident with assertion. Our own personal experiences suggest that put-offs and the skills of assertion are required at all stages of the influencing process. The reader is given examples of a continuum of human behaviour ranging from submissive to aggressive responses. The concept of win-win is discussed. The authors provide a structured framework for you to use to enhance your assertiveness. Assertive techniques are explored and the subject of saying no or challenging others is discussed.

CHAPTER 9: INTO ACTION

The final chapter is designed to pull all the previous chapters together by providing a summary of the salient points. It builds on the issues discussed in Chapter 3 and discusses the importance of making mental changes as a prerequisite to making change last. This should help you put the ideas of effective impact and influence into practice.

We now invite you to explore this book and hope that you can use the information we have distilled, developed and utilized as a foundation to enhance your influencing abilities.

ABOUT THE AUTHORS

Richard Hale is a practising management consultant and Director of Consulting with IMC Consulting, which is part of the internationally acknowledged business school, International Management Centres. Richard regularly works with such clients as Abbey National, Allied Domecq, Bass, Cellnet, Compaq and Holiday Inns. His early career was spent in training and development in GEC/Marconi Avionics and BSkyB, prior to joining Peter in 1992. Currently Richard is concluding doctoral research into the dynamics of mentoring relationships; some of this material is contained in this book. His other specialist interest is in the sphere of leadership development, in which he has pioneered the use of experiential training, including the use of the outdoors.

Dr Peter Whitlam is Chief Executive of International Management Centres, Europe. He is a truly international management consultant, working with such organizations as Andersen Consulting, BP, Coca-Cola, Lotus/IBM, Motorola and Nestlé. His early career was spent with Grand Metropolitan and the Burton Group, and most recently Coca-Cola and Schweppes Beverages. In 1988 he established his own business and was later joined by Richard Hale. Since that time both he and Richard have published numerous books covering all aspects of management. In particular, Peter has published cutting edge research into understanding how to achieve human potential. He currently specializes in individual executive coaching and mentoring for senior-level managers.

one

UNDERSTANDING INFLUENCE

On completion of this chapter the reader will:

- recognize the hierarchy of influence and be able to describe its four levels;
- have considered the major barriers to influence and explored ways in which these can be managed;
- have become familiar with the stages of the Model of Successful Influencing;
- have considered the issue of influencing in different cultural environments;
- have become aware of the two major strategic styles of influencing as well as having considered the major tactical options.

In this chapter we first describe what influencing is, giving you a definition and introducing you to the idea of a hierarchy of influence. Next we describe the barriers to influencing and enlarge upon the concept of the hierarchy of influence. One of the barriers to influencing can be the failure to utilize your own internal power or charisma. We outline the results of our research, which has explored the processes and behaviours of charismatic individuals or influencers. We then return to the theme of barriers to influence, in particular cultural barriers. Finally, we introduce you to two different influencing strategies, allowing you to consider how you normally tend to influence.

LEVELS OF **INFLUENCE**

Influencing may be defined in many different ways; however, for the purposes of our work we have defined it as follows: **the process of getting other people to accept our view(s) and feel OK about it; and for them to remain persuaded and enthusiastic enough to influence positively other people.**

Our definition aims to show how influence should not be seen as either a coercive or a manipulative process. By including a reference to remaining persuaded, we exclude the notion of using heavy-selling techniques or bullying. The ultimate sign of your success as an influencer is evidenced by the fact that the person will positively influence other people. What starts to emerge when you consider influence in this way is a hierarchy of influence, failure to manage which is a common blockage to effective influencing.

COMMON **BARRIERS**

Through our research and discussions with groups, many different barriers to effective influencing have been identified. Listed and expanded below are some of the more commonly described barriers.

FAILURE TO MANAGE THE HIERARCHY OF TRANSITIONS

Think about the definition of influence: it describes influencing essentially as a process of change. At this point it is worth reflecting on the stages that individuals and organizations go through when they are experiencing change. This is probably best illustrated by the following model, Figure 1.1.

The model suggests that when an individual is being influenced, under-going a change at a basic level, they are provided with information (**I know**). Above this they may be given new skills (**I can**). There is now a major step up to the next level of change (**I will**), which is concerned primarily with the individual's motivation. The difficulty here is that individuals may be motivated genuinely to do something, but shortly afterwards their priorities may change.

Storyboard: 'I thought we had agreed'

The executive quarterly reviews were arduous affairs usually held in a distant location over several days with all general managers making a presentation about their business performance.

The consultant sat patiently for three days waiting to give his presentation about the way to help the organization manage change. When invited, he had been informed that he would have two to three hours to present his recommendations. Unfortunately, as is often the way with these matters, all the managers exceeded their time allocations and it was clear that the consultant would not be getting his two to three hours.

Eventually his turn came, but by now it had been reduced to 20 minutes. Despite being a skilled presenter he was aware that he missed out an explanation of the underlying rationale for his recommendations for a change-orientation survey.

He noted that no questions were asked and that many of the audience seemed preoccupied with things like checking their flight tickets. Nevertheless all the individuals in the room seemed to be in general agreement and, when he finished, he stated that he would be contacting all general managers to discuss the specifics for their regions.

Four weeks later, having completed his design of the change-orientation instrument, he arrived back at the organization's HQ where he noted that he received a lukewarm reception. What agreement he thought he had got to move forward with the survey had been quickly put on hold.

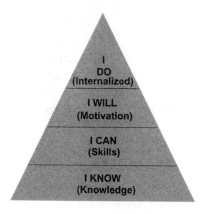

Figure 1.1 Failure to manage the hierarchy of transition

This real case illustrates two things: first, the level of influencing that had been achieved was only up to level 2, that is to say, the other people had only felt OK about it, but did not remain persuaded; and second, it typifies the problem of failure to manage the hierarchy in that initial motivation was not sustained. Ideally, to be successful, the consultant should have followed up the presentation quickly with individual meetings. It is often believed that imparting knowledge is influencing. It is not; but the belief is a barrier to many people's influencing.

The final level of the hierarchy of change (**I do**) is where the individual takes something 'on board', so that it becomes internalized; here influencing becomes self-perpetuating. This level represents real influencing. Throughout this book we help you to explore how you can achieve this level. We now continue to look at barriers to effective influencing.

LACK OF PREPARATION

Arguably this is the most common reason why we fail to influence others, and because of this we devote the next two chapters to exploring preparation and planning. It is important to realize that we influence others by what is important to them, not what is important to us. Lack of preparation is primarily about our failure to see things from the other person's point of view. Another equally important issue is that preparation is linked inextricably to the issue of confidence, without which we are likely to fail.

PSYCHOLOGICAL FACTORS

Influence is about change and real change comes from the inside. It is about getting another person or people to shift their view and engage in different behaviours. Consequently it is worthwhile being aware of the psychological stages that we all go through when we are faced with change. Recognizing these stages, each of which is a barrier, will help you to help others make a transition. These stages are as follows:

Denial

Initially individuals may deny that a problem or situation exists, the head in the sand approach. This stance need not necessarily alarm us. The only really effective way to deal with denial is by offering evidence; however, at this point we may find that the individual moves into the next stage of the psychological response to change.

Antagonism

On first examination antagonism may appear like denial but by careful listening we can quickly hear that the message we are receiving is not one of denial but more like, 'I don't want this. I don't need this. Leave me alone.' At this point it is useful to allow the other person to voice any concerns, as it is only when these have been expressed that they can be rebutted.

Another useful technique to use at this stage is closed or leading questions. By that we mean questions that provoke a simple response, yes or no, or questions that automatically suggest the required answer. In effect what we are trying to do is get the other person to agree with us.

Entrenched preconceived ideas held by the person you are trying to influence will clearly be a barrier to effective influencing. There is no easy way to overcome this problem other than by asking overtly for people to be open-minded or to suspend judgement. Where the problem seems to occur regularly, and when you have established dialogue with an individual, then a useful technique is to allow the person to criticize openly but only after he or she has provided at least three positive statements in support of what is being said. This approach brings some balance to the other person's antagonistic state, helping that individual and indeed you to realize that most issues are not as clear and polarized as they first appear.

Despite the difficulties of antagonism, by listening carefully we can often hear the person moving towards the next stage of the process.

Interest

Interest is really typified by the other person saying 'Come on; convince me', although rarely is the invitation so clear. The other person is now closer to adopting a much more open mind. This is the stage that really requires the application of verbal persuasive skills and is closely linked to the next stage.

Mental try-out

At this stage in the process the other person starts to visualize what is being described. Indeed, this is when we often use non-verbal behaviour aimed at helping that other person 'see' what we mean. Special attention should be given to listening carefully to what the other person is saying because at this point there may be clues about understanding, eg 'I see what you mean' or 'I can't see that working in our organization.'

Mental try-out always precedes the final stage which is when the individual actually does something.

Real-life try-out

The perceptual process when a person actually does something is important. If the process is perceived as positive then the person is likely to repeat or feel committed to it. However, when the individual undertakes something and feels that it is not particularly successful, then he or she is likely to return to the stage of antagonism. This is often about perception: the individual may have an expectation that is unrealistic, and consequently this may be an issue with which you need to confront the other person.

A further psychological issue, which can cause major blockages to the effectiveness of influence, is the relative status of the two people. This is highlighted by the example below, which is drawn from a real case.

Storyboard: Status barriers

Hans was a new graduate recruit who had joined an international electronics company as a graduate trainee direct from his university degree course. He was delighted to have been accepted onto the training scheme and the first week had been an interesting one; he had met a number of other trainees on the same programme and had enjoyed the graduate induction course.

It was the final day of the induction course and the company had arranged a drink and meal at its own social club. The idea was for the new recruits to mingle and to meet some of the older and more experienced employees. Hans was enjoying a drink at the bar with another employee whom he estimated was probably in his mid- to late fifties. The conversation proceeded along the following lines:

HANS: Yes the induction course has been really quite good fun. I've met a lot of people and they all seem good to work with. I even discovered that one of my old friends from school is on the same scheme. Anyway enough about me – what about you? How do you find it working here?

EMPLOYEE: Oh, I have always enjoyed it here – we obviously have our ups and downs though. The past year has been quite encouraging.

HANS: So I hear – can I get you another beer?

EMPLOYEE: Thanks a lot – I'll take a small one.

HANS: So what is your background then? Are you an engineer by training?

EMPLOYEE: Yes, electronic engineering. I studied in Germany and then got a lot of my early experience in the Far East.

HANS: How long have you been working here then?

EMPLOYEE: Oh, just over 20 years.

HANS: Well, it can't be that bad then – what do you do now?

EMPLOYEE: I'm the Chief Executive, actually.

HANS: Oh. . . no. . . I mean, I'm sorry. . . no, I don't mean I'm sorry about your job. . . Oh dear, I'm not expressing myself too well. . . how can I say. . . I'm sorry that I didn't know who you were.

At this point Hans, who until now had been communicating very effectively with someone whom he assumed to be of similar status, started to fall apart in terms of his communication and influencing skills. His voice started trembling, he became stuck for words and he started muttering and stumbling around.

The only reason for this was his knowledge that he was one of the most junior people and he was talking to the most senior manager in the organization. He had already proved his social skills and was making a good impression on the chief executive while his perception was that they were on a similar level. As soon as he became aware of the status differential he temporarily lost all of his social control and poise.

The above example highlights the principle of 'frames', the suggestion that everything we do is influenced by the frame or context in which we put it. Every interaction or discussion depends on a context for its meaning; that context is subject to an interpretation. In the example of the discussion above, as far as Hans was concerned at the start, the context was two employees of a broadly similar level having a drink and an informal conversation in a bar. When, however, he found out that he was talking to the chief executive, his frame changed dramatically. Suddenly the frame was of a formal interview situation where he perceived he was of considerably less value than the other person.

One way of dealing with this sort of situation, and this is a technique which particularly lends itself to dealing with intimidation and fear of others, is to deliberately 'reframe' the situation. So instead of Hans thinking of his colleague as a chief executive, he might reframe the situation and think of him as a family man who enjoys a social drink with his family and friends. It may sound as though we are suggesting we should move into the realms of fantasy, but this is a very practical approach which entertainers and major performers use to help them cope with situations which would otherwise be frightening. In a business context, it may be that you reframe a situation so that you picture the people you are trying to influence in less formal clothing, for example in a family role, or even try to picture what they were like as children. Many people, who discover a reframe that works for them, describe what a powerful yet simple technique reframing is. In many ways your ability to reframe will be partly determined by your powers of visualization and your ability to use imagery.

COMMUNICATION BARRIERS

We now list and describe the communication barriers when influencing.

Selective listening

By this we mean that people hear what they want to hear, rather than what is actually said. It is a common perceptual distortion, and can be managed easily by checking understanding or asking the other person to repeat something to you. We are naturally selective in our listening, and this is often a survival tactic. We are exposed to so much information, much of it through sound, that the only way to make sense of the world is through selective perception. Listening is likely to be more acute when something is of personal interest or, for that matter, a threat. Have you ever been in a crowded noisy room where it is difficult to pick out specifically what anyone is saying and then suddenly you hear someone on the opposite side of the room mention your name? That is selective listening operating at a subconscious level. The part of our brain that does the selection is called the reticular activating system. This network of cells, which extends from the central core of the brainstem to all parts of the cerebral cortex, only lets through into our conscious minds those things we have decided are important or of threat. People also filter out information more consciously, particularly when they are hearing things that they do not like.

Throughout the influencing process it is worth trying to identify whether the other person seems to be filtering out certain information. You may need to confront them about it. Similarly there is a danger that you too will listen selectively to what the other person has to say. We will look at personal listening skills later in the book.

Another contributory factor to our valuing or devaluing what is being said, or indeed to our not valuing the source of the information or the person who is transmitting that information, may be the use of jargon.

Use of jargon

Often language presents a significant barrier to influencing; and we are not referring simply to the national language spoken but also to the terminology and jargon that tend to pervade working life in most professions and disciplines. Stop and reflect upon the physiological description of selective listening given above (the reticular activating system). Did the use of what some might describe as jargon put you off, did it heighten your interest, or did it have no effect?

You will probably be able to anticipate or guess the likely language issues before meeting the person or people you are trying to influence. It is important to look out for the sort of words that are being used by them. For example when talking to engineers about how to select team members you may use words such as 'create a template against which you can compare people', and if talking to accountants on the same subject you may use language such as 'measure and assess the skills required'.

In most organizations and professions there are certain expressions and terms which are used more than others. One organization uses so many three-letter abbreviations to describe anything from procedures to job titles that it has published an internal book of what it refers to as TLAs! While you may question the value of developing such a secondary language, understanding the buzz words of those you are trying to influence can have significant advantages. It may be appropriate occasionally to echo the same terminology in order to encourage identification, though caution needs to be exercised in using this approach.

More often the problem is understanding the terminology used by people who are members of other groups than our own. In such a case it is imperative to question the other person as soon as possible to clarify meaning; the trick is to the commit such language and meaning to memory for the future. Conversely it is advantageous to recognize the jargon which you tend to use and to question whether the person you are attempting to influence will understand your 'language'.

One should recognize, however, that often jargon is used deliberately to create an impression of expertise as a way of influencing the other person. Some professions make an art form of this, converting the simplest issues into the most complex-sounding concepts. These may be presented in such a tone as to suggest that the person should understand what is meant and should not dare to ask for interpretation. If you sense this technique being used by others on you, try asking what is meant; you may be surprised pleasantly by the response!

PAUSE FOR **THOUGHT**

1. *What jargon do you use? Consider jargon that might be specific to the following groups you are involved with: professional; organizational;*

and peer group. Consider the people you attempt to influence; to what extent do you use terminology that may actually hinder the communication process? What alternative terminology could you use which might be more effective?

2. *Next consider the deliberate use of jargon and supposedly 'technical' terms. When might others have used this as an influencing technique on you? How effective was it? When have you used this approach on others? How effective was it?*

Saying too much

A frequent barrier to effective communication and influencing is overload. It has been shown that most people are able to retain between five and seven pieces of different information at the same time. Because of this it is worth presenting information in small quantities rather than in bulk. When received in bulk, the other person is likely to switch off.

This is in some way related to selective listening. It may be that people are selective in their listening because of the sheer amount of information coming at them. This issue has implications for how information should be presented to those we are trying to influence. It should be possible to summarize arguments, views and ideas succinctly. Overembellishment is likely to lead only to confusion. Review carefully the length, complexity and relevance of your message. This issue is particularly important when presenting written information.

ISSUES OF RECALL

Numerous studies have shown how quickly individuals forget what has been said or agreed. The graph in Figure 1.2 shows this most clearly.

Interestingly, immediately after an event the levels of recall at first increase. This is undoubtedly because our brains are still processing the data. However, the loss of recall is then dramatic.

Clearly this is an issue that needs to be managed when we are influencing others. We suggest that if you feel that you have successfully influenced someone, then try to do other things that will keep the issue at the forefront of their consciousness. This could include such things as dropping them an e-mail or sending them an article. As a principle this is particularly important when the issues being discussed are complex.

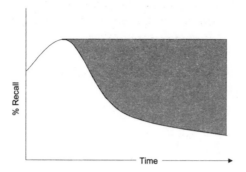

Figure 1.2 Poor levels of recall

LACK OF COMMITMENT

Commitment is about ownership. The only real way of gaining ownership is to have the other person involved. In effect this is about seeing the process of influencing as a two-way process rather than seeing the other person as a passive recipient. The critical skills here are those of listening and questioning. Likewise, when we are influencing others we should enter the process with a degree of flexibility rather than working to a fixed agenda or a specific output.

KEEPING ATTENTION

When influencing others it is useful to remember that the levels of attention will vary through the duration of the interaction. The graph overleaf, Figure 1.3, illustrates this point, highlighting that in the attention curve the greatest levels of attention are at the start and end of the interaction. Consequently these must be seen as critical stages of the process and are referred to as first impression and last impression.

The other important point to note is that throughout the course of the interaction there are periods when the attention curve rises and then falls. These peaks and troughs are the result of the person hearing (or seeing) something that they perceive as being of personal value or alternatively something that they consider as a threat. Clearly as part of our planning process we should try to highlight these issues and use them appropriately.

11

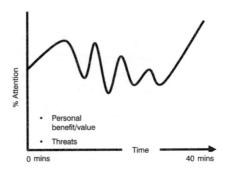

Figure 1.3 Exploiting the attention curve

Frequently the opportunity to influence is set within tight time constraints. The more pressure in terms of time, the less likely it is that a true pull type of influencing strategy will be possible; it is probable that more forceful approaches will have to be used when time is short. Alternatively it may be possible to make more time available and to question the validity of the time constraints being imposed.

UNDERUTILIZED POWER

Power may be seen as the opportunity to exercise influence on another person's actions. The power to influence is central to many human endeavours. We see various types of power being used in different ways to influence other people's actions; some may be categorized as follows:

Position or legitimate power

This is the power that comes from the position one person holds relative to the next person. In a military context this is about who has the most stripes on the arm, and in an organizational sense it relates to the job role and its position in the hierarchy. In extreme cases people using or abusing this source of power will use brute force in order to achieve results through others. As organizations are downsizing, delayering and reorganizing, the use of position power is clearly diminishing. As an influencing strategy the use of this sort of power may achieve results in the short term but it is likely to cause resentment if it is abused.

Coercive power

Coercion is about force. Coercive power can still be seen in some current organizational systems but, because of changing social values, the use of coercive actions is usually viewed in an extremely negative light. Consequently, where individuals use coercion, it will now tend to be covertly masked or hidden. It is frequently used by people who have some seniority in terms of position. A good example of this is the manager who wants to force co-operation of a peer but instead of being direct makes a comment such as, 'I am sure you will want to go along with this. It would be awful if we had to go to your boss to get this resolved.' Similarly there is the example of the bank manager who, in forcing the sale of an insurance policy on a customer says, 'We are keen to maintain our good relationship, particularly as we are supporting your overdraft.'

As an approach to influencing others, coercion may be effective in the short term but frequently the consequence is that the other person feels resentful and in the long term may fail to comply. Alternatively, if the balance of power between the two parties shifts then it is possible that the person who has been coerced in the past will seek to 'pay back' the coercer at a later date. So in the examples above the coerced manager, who ultimately may get promoted to another department, could be obstructive in his or her dealings with the old colleague; and the bank customer may move his or her account to another bank.

Information power

This is the power that stems from knowledge and is a category that should not be underestimated. Increasingly organizations are recognizing the power of information and knowledge-workers are selling their intelligence at a premium. In order to protect their organizational-knowledge power, employers will draw up contracts specifying that employees cannot take their corporate knowledge with them when they move to a new employer.

On an individual level one only has to demonstrate slightly more knowledge than the other person in order to hold the balance of power. For example, the employee who is in the personnel director's office and happens to see a memo about an imminent internal reorganization may then hold great information-power. This could be used in a number of ways: it could be traded for other information, it could be used to build an impression of being 'on the inside track' or it could be used to intimidate others.

Resource or reward power

Resource power stems from the possession or control of valued resources, which could be material or non-material, including anything that other people want or value highly. The manager who controls the head-count, the budget and overtime allocation has a great deal of resource power. Such power is not related necessarily to position; so the secretary who controls office layout, allocation of equipment and access to conference rooms may also hold a great deal of resource power.

Referent power

This is the power that people get from their formal positions and relationships with others. A typical example of this is a secretary who acts in the same distant or formal way as the boss in dealing with junior managers, such behaviour being based on an assumption of power derived from the boss. This power may or may not have been given to the individual. Where the power is abused, it stems from the individual acting as if he or she is able to control and influence the other person. Like most issues of power it can only be used successfully where the person being influenced allows it to take place.

Dynastic power

This power is similar to referent power inasmuch as it is the power that comes not from what you know or what you have, but from who you know. Unlike referent power the relationships will probably not be formalized, and will cross formal boundaries. An example of this is a junior member of staff who derives dynastic power from a social relationship with the chairman. In this example there is no formal relationship; any relationship that does exist may be based on some shared past common experience such as knowing the chairman socially through membership of a club or society.

A frequently used dynastic influencing strategy is to associate with someone who is respected by the other party. Consider the following interaction between a product supplier and a manager.

> SUPPLIER: It's good to see you again. It was only last week I was talking about some of the changes taking place in your department.
> MANAGER: Oh, were you?
> SUPPLIER: Yes, I was at the golf club with your chief executive; there are some interesting ideas being discussed at board level currently.

MANAGER: Mmm. . . I've heard a few rumours about changes.

SUPPLIER: Well, it seems no organization can avoid change. I was talking with your main competitor recently and they have some really innovative approaches.

What is important here is not so much what the supplier says but what is not said. The supplier actually has no position power over the client, but is making good use of dynastic power by implying close relationships with key people such as the chief executive and the main competitor. What the client does not know is that the supplier was actually carrying the chief executive's golf clubs; and in the discussion with the competitor he was bidding for business.

Expertise

As the role of experts becomes more important in organizations, so the power base is shifting from those who hold power traditionally because of their position, to those who may actually hold more junior positions. It is surprising how often, when someone has only expertise power, others will assume he or she holds position power. Again some people will make good use of perceived expertise to build a power base for influencing others. Techniques that capitalize on the use of expertise power, often with powerful results, include:

■ deliberately using jargon which the other person does not understand;
■ overtly assuming the other party will understand while actually knowing he or she will not;
■ quoting facts or figures;
■ referring to research and third parties.

We all use the above sources of power at different times, and many of us change our sources in different contexts. However, each of us will have our primary and secondary power sources, our personal preferences. Despite this, we should now consider a source of power that is available to us all, and in addition is capable of being improved dramatically as a way of influencing others.

Personal or charismatic power

Personal power is easier to recognize than to analyse. When asked to describe some of the characteristics of the most powerful influencers they know, people will frequently make comments such as:

15

- 'He just seems to have some quality I can't describe.'
- 'She's really strong in dealing with people but I don't know specifically what it is she does or how she does it.'
- 'He's got charisma – when he walks in the room people know it.'
- 'She seems to get people on her side.'

Personal power of this kind is often considered to be indefinable. Using powerful analytical behavioural techniques, we have studied the particular characteristics and skills such people demonstrate and as a result of this we have been able to develop the Model of Successful Influencing, which we believe describes the total influencing process and the skills associated with the process of influencing.

This model forms the basic structure for the book. We believe that successful influencing involves six process steps as described by the Model of Successful Influencing and that each step has associated competences.

THE MODEL OF SUCCESSFUL **INFLUENCING**

Each of the process steps is described below along with its associated competences. At this stage we need to highlight two issues. First of all the Model of Successful Influencing does not represent reality; we present it to you as a route map, a means of finding your way around.

Please note that we ask our readers to take the route map approach in a more pragmatic than literal way. Second, we do not suggest that each process step has unique competences. We do, however, suggest that each process step majors on specific competences. By focusing on the specific competences of influencing, managers we have worked with have proved that personal power or charisma is not simply an innate strength. It is something that can be developed through understanding and practice.

PREPARATION

This step is about being ready to influence, it is about being equipped with the right information and it is about being equipped with the right mind-set for influencing. The key competence for this first stage of the process is planning, in terms both of gathering information and of mental readiness. Development of these is explored in Chapters 2 and 3.

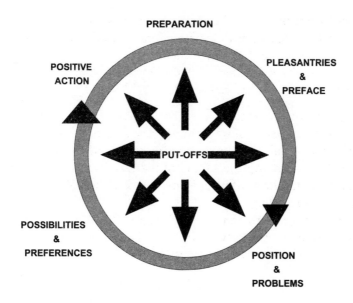

Figure 1.4 The Model of Successful Influencing

PLEASANTRIES AND PREFACE

This process step is about warming up the dialogue, developing the relationship and introducing the issue (the preface). The key competences are impact, rapport and gaining attention. These issues are explored in Chapter 4.

POSITION AND PROBLEMS

This stage in the process involves the thorough understanding of the other person's perspective. Key skills are questioning and listening, development of which is covered in Chapter 5. There is a need to discuss the difficulties or problems associated with the current position and, having agreed the need to tackle or overcome these problems, this prepares the ground for discussion of possible courses of action.

POSSIBILITIES AND PREFERENCES

At this stage a range of possible courses of action are discussed, leading to the actual preferred option being proposed.

POSITIVE ACTION

A key requirement in any influencing situation is to agree what action is going to be taken by both parties, but most importantly by the person who has been influenced. Sales people often talk about 'closing the sale' and this is the equivalent in the context of influencing. This is covered in Chapter 6.

PUT-OFFS

This stage of the process can occur at any time, hence it is positioned diagrammatically at the centre of the model. This stage is about dealing with confrontation and majors on the skills of assertion. Development of assertion is described in Chapter 8.

MANAGING CULTURAL **BARRIERS**

Having introduced you to the model that underpins this text, we now turn our attention to cultural difference, a further potential barrier to effective influencing. We draw on our international and multicultural experiences during various stages of the book, acknowledging that you too will be influencing in different cultural settings.

Cultural barriers can cause serious problems in an influencing situation. The Trompenaars research (1993) provides a useful basis for exploring this area, and is used throughout the book. By way of introduction to the cultural issues, we look at the contrasts between 'achievement'-oriented and 'ascription'-oriented cultures and the effect they have on influencing.

In an achievement-oriented culture, respect tends to be given primarily to those who have achieved through their own efforts almost regardless of issues such as age and experience. By contrast, in an ascriptive-oriented culture, the main focus of respect is the position people hold in the hierarchy, which is largely determined by age and experience. Status is ascribed due to the position, level, age and even family background of the person. Scandinavian, British and North American cultures tend to be more achievement-oriented whereas Middle Eastern and Asian cultures tend to be more ascriptive. These differences clearly affect the influencing situation in a crucial way as the issues tend to surface when someone from one culture is attempting to influence a person from another culture. So if a young dynamic self-made man from the United States travels to the Middle East to do business with a senior and significantly older team of Arabs there could be immediate credibility problems. He would do well to emphasize his years of experience rather than that he is the youngest senior executive in the organization. He might gain more kudos by emphasizing that he is related to the chairman in his organization than by talking about his personal achievements.

Similarly a key variable between cultures is that of 'individualism' as opposed to 'collectivism'. In an individualist culture, the main focus of attention and indeed power is usually the individual. In a collectivist culture, where the group is considered to be more important than the individual, decisions tend to be made on a group basis. In the preceding example, the young manager's instinct may tell him to target the decision-maker in order to strike a deal, whereas a more appropriate approach would be to recognize openly the various levels of manager based on their titles and to show some patience in awaiting decisions.

Another principle to recognize as being of major importance in some cultures is that of allowing other people to save face. In, for instance, an ascriptive culture the more junior members of a team are likely to offer close support to their seniors and provide answers and assistance privately if they fear there is a danger of the senior members being embarrassed. They will then be quite content for the seniors to take the praise because this respects the hierarchy. As someone attempting to influence in this environment it may be necessary to play the same game and realize that, even though a senior person is incorrect or wrong in their understanding of a situation, it would be more appropriate to confront that person privately afterwards than in front of peers or subordinates.

It is clearly difficult to give specific advice regarding what to say and do when influencing across cultures; what is important is to try to assess the cultural ground rules or norms before, or during the early stages of, a discussion. Whilst it will be inappropriate to change one's own culturally influenced behaviour radically, it may be appropriate to make modifications and accept that there are differences. These chameleon-like qualities are becoming increasingly important in influencing others successfully in an increasingly global world. Now we highlight two different strategies for influencing, before exploring process and skills using the Model of Successful Influencing outlined previously. Finally in this introduction to influencing, we introduce the concept of influencing strategies.

TWO DIFFERENT INFLUENCING **STRATEGIES**

It is worth recognizing the two major strategic types of influencing. Exploring these differences will provide valuable contextual information for you, helping develop further your understanding of influence.

Hard strategies

Hard strategies are often used in traditional negotiations. With this approach the person who is trying to influence another usually starts by making a demand that is exceptionally high. This is a shock tactic. Once such a demand had been made, an alternative lesser demand is made and the recipient psychologically breathes a sigh of relief. 'Psychological relief' is widely used in advertising where the company creates an anxiety in the other person and then provides the relief, ie their product.

Soft strategies

With this approach the influencer aims to get a foot in the door and gain minor concessions that ultimately move on to greater concessions. This is the approach most widely used when influencing others in organizations. It relies on the concept of 'uncertainty reduction', the fact that people like to be able to predict their environment and thus feel as if they are in control.

There are also two main tactical ways of influencing: the central route and the peripheral route.

The central route

When the audience has the ability and is motivated to pay attention to the argument then the most effective tactics to use are logic, rationality and compelling argument.

The peripheral route

By contrast, if the audience are not motivated to pay attention then it is important to pay attention to issues like the environment, the duration of the interaction and the personality and style of the influencer. In reality most influencing takes place using aspects from both styles.

CONCLUSION

In this introductory chapter we have developed ideas of what influencing is. We have introduced you to the concept of a hierarchy of influence and explored the barriers to influencing. We have looked at an influencing process model, the Model of Successful Influencing, and highlighted the competences linked to that model. Finally we have raised some issues with regard to influencing in different cultures and presented ideas on approaches to influencing. Before moving on we invite you to consider the questions below and plan how you intend to enhance your influencing interactions based on the information you have read.

PAUSE FOR **THOUGHT**

1. *What are the most common barriers that I experience when influencing others?*
2. *How can these barriers be managed?*
3. *What issues relating to cultural diversity do I need to consider?*
4. *When influencing others, which of the two strategies do I prefer to use?*
5. *When dealing with others, how can I enhance things like my expertise, attractiveness and power?*

two

PREPARATION: INFORMATION GATHERING

At the completion of this chapter the reader will:

- recognize the importance of understanding perspectives and be able to use a perspective specification as part of planning and preparation;
- have examined the 'push' and the 'pull' styles of influencing and learnt about the importance of trying to understand the other person's perspective;
- be able to use a questioning framework aimed at ensuring complete understanding of the position and problem in anticipation of an influencing situation;
- know the importance of understanding the other person's values and style as a prerequisite to achieving lasting change.

INTRODUCTION

Below we explore what is meant by preparation and planning. We consider the issue of influencing in the context of preparing, before introducing the idea that understanding perspectives is critical to effective influencing. Linked to this idea we touch on why you need to consider the other person's values. We then give you ideas for influencing people with different styles and more insights into cultural differences.

In the previous chapter, we looked at the Model of Successful Influencing in which we described six key steps that successful influencers appear to take in the process of influencing others. The model provides a focus for the key parts of the process. It may not, however, mirror the reality you experience since discussions are less likely to move from step to step in a predictable manner. We highlighted each of these six stages and described how each process stage demands certain competences. We focused on these competences or skills, knowledge and understanding in order to provide you with the best opportunity for improving your influencing performance.

We will now turn our attention in detail to the stage of **preparation**, the first stage that draws upon, in particular, the competence of gathering information. We define preparation as: **actions which indicate a degree of mental and physical readiness for a particular influencing situation. This includes recognizing the information needs and perspectives of the other party; and being able to demonstrate preparation to that person by our words or actions.**

So good preparation for an influencing situation could mean thinking through in advance what the other person is likely to be thinking, and assembling that information in order to maximize your influencing effectiveness. It is also advantageous actually to discuss with the other person what you are looking to achieve from the interaction. But preparation is not just about knowing you have prepared effectively; like so many of the influencing skills it is about showing, through your behaviour, that you are prepared. How, for instance, might you demonstrate that you are prepared for an important presentation? You might do it by arriving in good time, setting the furniture out in a particular way, having materials laid out on the table, having an introductory slide showing on the screen and approaching the guests as they enter to introduce yourself. All of these actions actively demonstrate preparation. Equally, preparation could be shown simply through demonstration that you know your subject. How often have you been in a meeting where you have reached a stalemate because the other person did not have to hand all the information or details required?

It could be argued that preparation is not always possible because we cannot always anticipate what to expect of the person we are trying to influence or because there is simply very little time to prepare. In part we would agree with this line of thought; however, for the purposes of this chapter we will assume that we do know when we are going to try to influence someone. Often influencing opportunities arise unplanned and in these situations it is important to be able to think on one's feet, but it is still possible to apply some of the same disciplines of preparation albeit in a less formal way.

We will look at a practical technique of preparation for information gathering, known as the perspective specification. This technique can help with the common problem of not being able to predict the other person's approach. In a similar way we will make reference to the importance of managing data in the preparation phase. This, we will show, can be done by the use of an information specification.

The key principle of successful influencing which is relevant to every stage of the Model of Successful Influencing is: **You cannot influence what you do not understand.** This statement puts a focus on the competence of planning, of gathering and developing information, which we suggest is critical before engaging in the influencing process. In order to maximize the chances of success, and to be able to understand issues such as the other person's background, values, motivation, experiences and objectives, planning is required. It is important to remember that we influence others best when we use a style familiar to them. This also means being aware of significant cultural differences particularly if working in an international environment. We will explore this issue now. We invite you to enter the world of planning to influence by asking you first to consider the style of the person you are trying to influence and the style you need to adopt for a given situation.

UNDERSTANDING THE STYLE OF **OTHERS**

A common trap that you may fall into, when attempting to influence others, is to work from your own frame of reference or values rather that of the other party. This usually leads to what might be described as a push rather than a pull style of influence. With a push style of influence the strategy adopted is to be clear about your own argument and then aim to impose your views on the other person. This is clearly a forceful or even aggressive approach; if the other person disagrees or holds a different opinion from yours then you will block it with the same degree of force used in presenting it. In this familiar situation a game of influencing 'tennis' takes place. Arguably there may be some situations where this approach is appropriate such as when:

- there is no time to use a more persuasive approach and fast decision-making is needed, for instance on matters of safety or security where you are absolutely sure that you are correct;
- unpopular decisions need to be taken such as cost-cutting or the implementation of unpopular rules. Even in this situation it is important to consider carefully the style of influencing and the requirement to listen to the views of the other party;

■ the other person is using an aggressive or forceful approach, making no effort to listen. Even in this situation it may be possible to adopt a pull approach rather than having to push against the other person's arguments, but sometimes the only way to hold back the force of the other person is to start with an equally forceful stance.

To continue the theme of sporting analogies, American football provides a good example of the push-type approach. Frequently we see the footballer running straight at the other team and being met by the opposition player running equally fast heading for a direct collision. Often it is brute force that will win the day, which is fine if you are bigger and stronger than the other person. It is hardly surprising that the players need the help of substantial padding and painkillers! The football approach is about meeting others head on, presenting your argument as forcefully as they do and emphasizing the differences.

The pull approach, however, can be likened best to the sport of judo, which relies on skill, guile and when appropriate force. Most important of all judo relies on being able to sense the movements, actions, force and direction of the other person. Interestingly this is the reason that visually impaired or blind judo players often make such good contestants; they compensate for their inability to see the opposite player by focusing on feeling their actions and intentions. Losers are thrown or beaten by their own strength and force which is used against them by the winner pulling them in the direction they were already travelling and applying often subtle techniques and twists.

In an influencing context the pulling approach means sensing and trying to understand where the other person is coming from. It means seeing things through his or her eyes, and then deciding on the tactics for influencing. It is an effective strategy, using someone's own arguments and values to bring about persuasion. Clearly you need to think about the style of influence that is appropriate for a given situation as part of your initial preparation.

EXPLORING **PERSPECTIVES**

Understanding the perspective of the other person can be especially difficult if you hold strong and opposing views. The instinctive reaction is to meet force with force; however, attempting to understand the other person's perspective can be a very revealing and effective way of moving forward. Frequently, different people will look at the very same subject or situation from quite different perspectives. A helpful analogy is used by Calvert *et al* in the book *First Find Your Hilltop* where it is suggested that each of us views a situation from our own unique perspective or 'hilltop', based on our own experiences, motives, values, opinions and attitudes. The important skill is identifying the nature of the other person's hilltop. Arguably what we need to do is to come down off our own hilltop and go up onto the other's hilltop, as only by so doing could we be aware of how they really see things. This is not actually possible; however, a useful questioning technique for helping us understand the other person's perspective is three-level questioning, which we explore in Chapter 5. As a diagnostic technique it works when we have contact with the other person. If we do not have such contact, it becomes important to attempt to anticipate the other's perspective or view. A practical technique which can be used at this stage of early preparation and information gathering is the perspective specification.

THE PERSPECTIVE SPECIFICATION

To draw up a perspective specification you first need to be able to identify the different parties involved. This may sound obvious, but there is frequently more than one person to influence, and politically it is crucial to recognize who the key decision-makers are. Consider, for example, an internal consultant attempting to secure a commitment for specific actions. While the actions may concern one internal customer, for example, the finance manager, other key players in the decision to proceed may be the IT manager and the departmental manager or end user.

On a similar note take the case of the university lecturer talking at a careers convention. The lecturer, who is in the influencing role, may be trying to persuade a number of quite different potential customers of the strengths of the university: students, schoolteachers and parents.

A framework for constructing a perspective is provided in Table 2.1. As stated in our introduction, you will learn more through engaging with the ideas presented. You are therefore encouraged to think about an influencing situation you are involved in or a historical influencing situation. Apply the framework in order to develop a clearer understanding of the perspectives operating.

As guidance, the different parties are named at the head of the columns of the perspective specification form. The different sections of each column are completed after trying to see the situation from the different perspectives of each person. The important matter is the discipline of attempting to

Table 2.1 Perspective specification

How I see the problem/situation	How .... sees the problem/situation	How .... sees the problem/situation

see things through the other person's eyes; using this approach in your preparation will drastically enhance your influencing effectiveness.

Clearly at this early stage it is not possible to predict with pinpoint accuracy the position of the other person, but by using the discipline of a perspective specification you are likely to reduce the number of unexpected surprises and awkward questions once into the influencing discussion.

UNDERSTANDING AND MANAGING **INFORMATION**

Understanding the other person's perspective is a critical preparatory activity in the process of influencing. In a similar way it may be beneficial to consider the information that you are using as the basis of your approach to influencing. This is particularly important where the issues are complex.

In these circumstances it can be helpful to structure the preparatory analysis by the use of an information specification. With this technique we first ask ourselves what we really know for sure about the person or situation. This structured approach can be further enhanced by considering what we know, as well as what we do not know, about the 7Ms: money, market, manpower, methods, machines, materials and minutes (see Table 2.2). Of course not all these criteria may be appropriate or necessary, but they are helpful in structuring our thinking in complex situations. We provide you with the framework below and again ask you to apply the model to a past, current or forthcoming influencing situation.

Table 2.2 Building a questioning framework

	Known	**Unknown**
Money		
Manpower		
Market		
Materials		
Machines		
Methods		
Minutes		

A final practical and useful tool for assessing the current situation is that of force field analysis. In preparation, this tool helps you identify the perceived barriers in an influencing situation. The force field analysis model works on the basis that any situation is an equilibrium of opposing forces, forces pushing for change and resisting forces. If you can identify these forces and estimate their strengths in advance of the influencing situation you will be well prepared. Take for example the force field diagram in Figure 2.1 that highlights the forces at work in a pay review.

A number of forces favouring a pay rise have been identified and a number of forces against. Having identified these forces, you can target how you are going to try to influence the situation. Can you increase some forces or weaken others in order to get a pay rise? Using force field analysis in preparation for an influencing situation helps you prepare your approach, taking many factors into account.

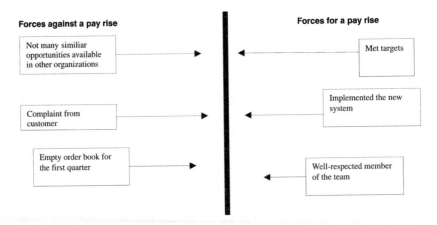

Figure 2.1 Forces in a pay review

We now move on to consider how you can prepare for an influencing situation by trying to identify and work with the other person's values.

RECOGNIZING CRITICAL **VALUES**

In preparation, it is certainly beneficial to try to identify the underlying motives of the people you are attempting to influence and to consider their basic values or driving forces. We all are driven by a hard core of values, probably numbering no more than a few, and these values then fuel our beliefs, attitudes, choices and behaviours.

While it is helpful to be able to identify and anticipate the behaviours and actions of the other person, it can be even more advantageous to be able to identify fundamental values. This is because most of our behaviours tend to be driven by core values. For example, if you are trying to influence a person who holds a core value of independence for the individual, then this should affect your influencing strategy. Say you are trying to persuade this person to take on a task that you want to delegate. To influence effectively, you will need to emphasize that the task is one which he or she will be able to tackle with a strong level of individual choice as to how it is done.

Examples of fundamental values might include:

- the importance of education;
- family values;
- the profit motive;
- belief in God or an overall power;
- personal responsibility;
- fairness and equality;
- the work ethic.

Each of our core values may in itself consist of numerous related beliefs. For example, if we hold the importance of education as a core value, this could mean that we have a belief in the notion of an individual's potential to achieve, or in education being about wealth creation or physical or mental well-being. In turn, we may have hundreds, if not thousands, of attitudes related to these beliefs. Using the education example, we could well have an attitude towards higher education, or towards the use of technology in education, or towards access to kindergarten education for all.

Interestingly, organizations also have values and frequently they consider what these values should be and overtly state them. Often they can be identified from written sources such as the mission statement or vision statement. For example, Steve Jobs of Apple states: 'Our goal has always been to create the world's friendliest, most understandable, most usable computers – computers that empower the individual' (Weyer, 1994).

McDonald's are well known for their key values of quality, service, cleanliness and value, and they clearly attempt to work to these values consistently across locations. Hewlett Packard commit their values to writing in 'The HP Way', a document available to all employees.

A more accurate judgement of organizational values might be drawn from discussion with employees at various levels. These values are essentially about the culture of the organization or 'the way we do things around here', and even if they are not openly stated, then there is no doubt that they will exist. Organizational values might include, for example:

■ dignity for the individual;
■ integrity;
■ loyalty;
■ innovation;
■ the profit motive;
■ contribution to society.

From an influencing point of view, there is a lot to gain by successfully identifying the core values of the individual and the organization. The primary benefit is that you will be able to use the values of the other person or organization as part of the influencing process. You are likely to be significantly more persuasive by using arguments which use the other person's value system rather than trying to impose your own values on them. Let's consider some examples that highlight this principle.

Storyboard: Using what is important to other people

Susan is a new recruit to a conservative consumer-products organization and has considerable experience of working in a fast-moving high-technology US corporation. She has joined in the role of product manager to try to bring about significant product changes and to enhance the image of the organization's brands in the market-place. She is currently trying to influence a senior manager, Charles, to gain commitment to major innovations in the use of information technology systems and marketing. She has analysed the organizational values and also the personal values of the senior manager as follows:

Organizational values: Cost containment, conservative approach, fear of change

---

Personal values: Security, safety, caution, concern about risk-taking

> SUSAN: Clearly the important issue, Charles, is to continue to build on some of the developments which have been occurring over the last few years.

Tactically this is a good approach; having identified that Charles is a cautious man, she positions her ideas as part of the changes that have been taking place anyway. Selection of words is important; she talks about 'building on' rather than changing. Her use of Charles's name can be a strong influencing technique, but a word of caution is appropriate: if this is overdone it can be transparent, even irritating.

> CHARLES: Yes, but I really think we need to make sure we don't move too fast; I've seen too many other organizations make sweeping changes only to have to revert to the tried and tested methods eventually.

This response does not come as a total surprise to Susan who is prepared for the cautious approach. Fortunately she has thought of some possible responses.

> SUSAN: I agree. I too have seen some examples of organizations that have attempted some quite revolutionary approaches to branding; many have fallen into some of the classic traps such as not analysing likely market response. Maybe we should look at some of the lessons that can be learnt and at the same time look at some of the success stories.

Although this response may seen innocuous Susan is using a number of effective influencing techniques. She has recognized that with Charles a directly forceful or hard sell approach will not work. She works with his style and values. She starts by agreeing with his objection, which in itself is a legitimate approach; by agreeing in part she openly shows support and may draw Charles closer to her when he may be expecting more of a confrontation. What she then does is use the same argument in support of her own ideas by suggesting they look at lessons learnt. This is likely to appeal to Charles who is cautious and conservative. She uses a tentative word in 'maybe' which gives Charles the opportunity to build on her suggestions rather than feel that he is being railroaded.

The key principle in the above example is that, to be effective in an influencing context, it is essential to try to anticipate matters arising from the personal style and underlying values of the other person. You need to suggest that you are giving consideration to the values of the person you are influencing. What clues has he or she given you from your previous interactions? Admittedly we are not always in a position to identify these issues in advance of the meeting, for example, when meeting a person for the first time.

As previously stated, it is even more important to be able to identify the same factors through a process of skilful questioning and observation in the early part of the interaction. We will cover questioning and listening skills in Chapter 5, these being the fundamentals of the positioning and problems stage of the influencing process, the Model of Successful Influencing.

We now develop this idea of understanding the person you are trying to influence by identifying some typical styles. Differing value bases drive these styles. If you feel that you know the individual you are trying to influence reasonably well, you might like to consider their style against the four key categories we identify below. If you are able to categorize the other person in terms of our definitions then some suggested influencing methods are provided.

We also consider the situation where you are the manager attempting to influence a subordinate who has a predominant style and also the situation where you are the subordinate attempting to influence your manager. This is not about mimicking the other person in an ape-like way; you are likely to be more persuasive if you can recognize their preferred style and adapt your style to theirs rather than imposing your style on them.

STYLE 1: SUPPORTIVE

People who fit the supportive style of behaviour are likely to believe in the importance of personal relationships. They will tend to approach problem solving from a collaborative point of view and will be supportive to other people who are less experienced. They are likely to enjoy working with others and will share responsibility and resources readily. Trust is an important issue for supportive people and they are likely to build long-term relationships.

How to influence a person with a supportive style

When influencing people with this sort of style it is important to stress the worthwhile nature of long-term causes. It may be appropriate to emphasize the relationship between your objective and their personal development. An effective technique to use with people who have a supportive style is to ask for their help in tackling a problem. Be careful of criticism of such people; they are particularly likely to fear ridicule and failure.

How to manage someone with a supportive style

It is important when managing a subordinate who has a predominantly supportive style to give recognition to his or her ideas, achievement and contribution. It will help to provide opportunities for him or her to work with or alongside others. Sharing information and being open will help in the relationship. When setting goals and targets they should involve both parties having a say, and the manager should make opportunities available for the subordinate to achieve these targets.

How to influence a boss with a supportive style

If your boss demonstrates a predominantly supportive style, it will be important to demonstrate your value and contribution to the organization. Sincerity and honesty will be particularly respected and it will be better to admit mistakes and seek help rather than cover them up. Willingness to participate in team activities and tasks is important.

STYLE 2: COMPETITIVE

The competitive style is one where the person tends to rely on authority and position-based power, and approaches tasks in a strongly competitive manner. The main aim of the competitive person is to achieve results, challenge others and to get on with doing things.

How to influence a person with a competitive style

Methods of influencing competitive people should emphasize the opportunities being offered to them and ways in which they can raise their personal profile. If it is possible to give authority to them then they are likely to respond favourably. Equally, the competitive person is likely to respond well to direct approaches and will be intolerant of 'woolly' approaches which may be seen as weakness.

How to manage someone with a competitive style

When managing a subordinate with a predominantly competitive style it will be necessary to influence by giving challenges and providing autonomy and individual responsibility. It is important to give recognition for achievements. It may be necessary to define clearly the demarcation of the role so that this person does not undermine or encroach on the responsibilities of others. However, it will be appropriate to give him or her the opportunity to use initiative within the given boundaries. It may on occasion be a requirement to spar on an equal basis.

How to influence a boss with a competitive style

It will help to take a direct approach when dealing with a boss with this style. This means demonstrating your capability and showing independence, but not being afraid to recognize the boss as a resource to draw on for assistance when required. When you are confident that you are right it may help if you stick to your views and meet objections head-on. This sort of boss will not appreciate servile behaviour, though subordinates do often take a submissive stance in dealing with a competitive manager. He or she will enjoy a challenge and the cut and thrust of a strong argument. When influencing a competitive person, you will sometimes need to mirror the direct and straight-talking approach.

STYLE 3: RESTLESS

The restless style is often seen in people who enjoy change and thrive on opportunities to be in the spotlight. Typically a restless style can be recognized by a tendency to be optimistic, active and sociable. This sort of person tends to enjoy dealing with new and different people and situations.

How to influence a person with a restless style

Generally it is preferable to emphasize the benefits of change when influencing someone with a predominantly restless style. He or she is likely to respond positively to new ideas, which is in contrast to the consolidative style described below. It will be effective to stress excitement and emotion associated with proposals.

How to manage someone with a restless style

If you are managing a subordinate who has a mainly restless style, it will help to take a flexible approach and to accept that this sort of person will respond better to variety than to routine tasks. To influence a restless person, offer supportive feedback and do not underestimate the impact of humour. Routines, firm schedules and close supervision are unlikely to be effective management strategies.

How to influence a boss with a restless style

If your boss has a restless style then the most effective responses as a subordinate will tend to emphasize eagerness and positive open attitudes to new ventures and products. Be wary of going into too much detail when explaining things. This sort of boss will tend to have a short attention span. Key competences will be the ability to make an impact quickly and to express oneself succinctly and clearly. You may offer to take on some of the more routine responsibilities in order to relieve your boss of these matters.

STYLE 4: CONSOLIDATIVE

The consolidative style tends to be biased towards order, routine and detail. A consolidative person will be comfortable with policy and doing things which are in the best interests of the organization or authority. This will often mean a suspicion of change and a preference for consistency.

How to influence a person with a consolidative style

The key to influencing someone with a consolidative style is to demonstrate a careful and cautious approach. Clearly Charles in the storyboard above has a predominantly consolidative style; we saw how Susan recognized this and adapted her approach accordingly, rather than relying on the more competitive approach which would have worked in her previous organization.

How to influence a boss with a consolidative style

If your boss has a consolidative style then you will need to be careful in making recommendations for change. A useful tactic is to stress how your recommendations are similar to or build on historical methods and systems. Arguments will be more persuasive if they stress conformity and logic, and are backed up by example. When attempting to influence it is better to be respectful of organizational norms or standards and it is important to be well prepared and have relevant facts and information to hand. This sort of boss will want to be confident that you have explored all possible options before agreeing to your proposals.

How to manage someone with a consolidative style

A perceptive manager will allocate certain types of responsibility to a consolidative subordinate; these will be tasks involving high levels of detail and planning. This sort of person will tend to be frustrated by changes which are made part way through projects. They will need time to make considered decisions rather than being rushed or pressurized. They will put a big emphasis on being treated fairly and will prefer a pragmatic managerial style.

Often national or cultural differences influence the underlying values of the individual and organization. We consider the fascinating subject of cultural differences below.

EXPLORING CULTURAL **DIFFERENCES**

The danger of talking about cultural differences in general terms is that we may fall into the trap of stereotyping people and nationalities. Nevertheless the issue needs to be taken into account in your preparation if you are going to be successful at influencing in multicultural settings. If we try to identify generally applicable rules regarding what you should or should not do or say when you are meeting with someone from, for instance, Germany, the United States, Japan or the Middle East, then there is a real risk of getting it wrong. Cultural issues are not this clear-cut and there will always be individuals who disprove the rule; so tread carefully.

There has been some interesting research into the subject of cultural differences, not least that conducted by Fons Trompenaars as published in his book *Riding the Waves of Culture* (1993); we use his research as a basis for exploring influence in differing cultural settings. He has studied cultural differences with an emphasis on international cultures. It is interesting when considering this subject to consider whether your organization or that of the person you are attempting to influence has a culture which fits a particular type. After all, culture is about norms for how things are done and organizations have norms just as nations do. Trompenaars defined a number of contrasts in terms of cultural differences. Here we will look at the contrast between universalism and particularism and how this relates to the preparation stage of the influencing process.

The universalist tends to be a clear-cut approach to business and the focus is on sticking to codes of conduct, rules, regulations and previously established practices. In a particularist culture, the relationship is more important than the contract; it is considered important to allow relationships to develop over time and informality is acceptable, even encouraged.

While it is wrong to make sweeping generalizations, you may recognize these differences if you have worked in the hard-nosed environment of a universalist US or northern European organization. Equally you may recognize the particularist culture in southern European or Middle Eastern relationships.

In an influencing situation, it is worth while considering the nature of the culture of the person you are trying to influence. In a universalist culture you will need to have key facts and figures to hand and it will be essential to know the background to the situation. You will need to know who else has been involved and what are the accepted ways of doing business. It may be necessary to use forceful approaches so make sure you are aware of where you stand legally. Before meeting it could be advisable to write formally, to clarify the agenda and objectives, and to do so again afterwards to confirm what was agreed.

In a particularist culture, while this level of preparation may turn out to be equally appropriate, it will be just as important to display flexibility and not to appear shocked if the 'goal posts are moved' and the rules seem to change as discussions evolve. This is not to underplay the importance of preparation, but it is a matter of style; the trick is to be prepared but to show willingness to adapt and to work on building a good relationship. And do not be deceived if you come from a universalist culture and the other person, from a particularist culture, appears to be wandering off the subject. It does not mean necessarily that he or she is ill prepared; it could simply be that time is being allowed for getting to know you.

In this chapter we have considered a number of different techniques for planning and gathering information that will help you in the face-to-face influencing situation. The overall message is that the importance of planning cannot be overplayed. It is the key that unlocks the door to the pleasantries stage of the Model of Successful Influencing.

Having done all you can in terms of initial preparation, it is now worth thinking a little more about the importance of your psychological readiness for influencing.

three

PREPARATION: MENTAL READINESS

By the end of this chapter the reader will:

- understand the enormous power of the mind and the apparently boundless potential we have to improve our performance;
- recognize that meaningful change starts inside us and works its way out rather than starting outside and working in;
- know we need to consider changing our thinking before or at the same time as we start changing our behaviour. We should not leave this process to chance;
- understand that perception is reality. There is only one truth, the way I see things. This may be different from your truth;
- see that our self-image is the product of our inner dialogue and understand the role of 'experts' and their influencing on the way we see ourselves;
- understand that, once developed, our self-image controls the way we behave by acting as a 'comfort zone', and that we do the things that align with our self-image;
- appreciate that mental practice and rehearsal actually improve physical performance;
- recognize that as individuals we move towards and become like what we think about. The more we think about success, the more we are likely to achieve it, and conversely the more we think of failure, the more likely we are to achieve it!

INTRODUCTION

Here we explore the importance of your mind-set before an influencing situation. We believe and practise the idea of change coming from within. This chapter explores human potential, the issue of learning and change, self-fulfilling prophecies and visualization. Putting these ideas and concepts into practice as preparation for influencing is the key to making you a successful influencer. In short, this chapter is all about how you can gear yourself up psychologically to be an effective influencer; it asks you to take the ideas and concepts and to reflect on your mental readiness for influencing.

It may sound strange, but many people are 'beaten' even before they have shaken the hand of the person they are about to influence. This is not caused necessarily by lack of preparation, but is more likely to be caused as a result of their negative self-talk or thinking processes. Consequently this chapter explores these issues, helping you to understand just what you can do to increase the likelihood of success.

Our research has shown that by controlling different aspects of our mental processes (which we call 'metacognition'), it is possible to bring about significant movement towards the achievement of better influencing and the achievement of personal goals and objectives.

THE POWER **WITHIN**

For thousands of years philosophers have pondered the nature and scope of our minds, yet the major developments in our real knowledge have come probably within the past couple of decades. Our understanding may be still in its infancy, a point that appears to be supported by the numerous different ideas and theories existing. For example, many have described the structure of the brain and there are vastly varying accounts as to its latent potential. We feel that this in itself is not that important; what is important is that it is generally recognized that the brain is made up of an enormous number of neurones or nerve cells. One of the functions of these cells is to record and then store or imprint experiences or data. These experiences may ultimately be capable of recall from our memory into our conscious arena; however, without doubt this retrieval will involve some level of distortion. For example, many remember only the pleasant aspects of a time long ago.

Another area of general agreement appears to be that most individuals do not begin to exploit their true potential. In part this seems to be due to the actual size of the brain, with its possibly endless number of different permutations. This limit to potential appears to be related to aspects of our beliefs and attitudes.

The brain can be likened to the hard disk on a computer, a limited metaphor which nevertheless serves the purpose of explanation. Like the computer, the brain records information without being concerned about whether that information is, for example, fact or fiction. The brain just records the sensory inputs. Here the similarity ends because the brain records information through the process of perception. The consequence of this is, in short, that people act in accordance with their beliefs and values, which are a kind of prerecorded database influencing our perception of the world, our feelings, our choices, our beliefs and values and, further, our behaviours.

Remember, influencing is about a sustained change to someone's perspective and behaviours. To be effective, you need to consider the psychological concepts we describe below.

INSIDE **OUT**

What is learning? Clearly there are many definitions; we would define learning as a lasting change of behaviour resulting from practice or experience. This sounds very much like influencing, which indeed it is.

Like most who make a living out of developing the potential of others within organizations, we have debated the strengths and weaknesses of traditional skills development programmes. Through careful programme design our efforts seemed to be getting good levels of transference or application of skills from the classroom to the working environment. On closer examination we were somewhat startled to discover that the problem of transference still existed. When monitoring past participants over a period of one year after attending a traditional skills development programme we found that there was a dramatic loss in that time in their ability to apply successfully the newly acquired skills. Indeed, the initial study suggested that after 12 months only 6 per cent of individuals had achieved any significant lasting change of behaviour.

There may of course be many reasons or contributing factors for this; however, further questioning of these individuals suggested that many of the barriers to the successful application of the new skills were primarily psychological in nature. Included in this were the following reasons for poor application:

- the negative influence of other people;
- 'not really seeing myself as being able to behave in that way';
- having beliefs that were inappropriate to applying the new skill, such as 'I've never been good at dealing with difficult situations';
- lack of personal motivation;
- inappropriate self-image.

This in itself should not have been surprising as most traditional skills training programmes tend to avoid the issue of developing mental processes, or mention them only as an afterthought.

These findings brought us to the conclusion that in order to produce lasting and sustained behavioural change, particularly in the area of influencing skills, we needed to address skill development and the issues of internal mental processes simultaneously. This can be explained best by Figure 3.1.

This model shows that behaviour, 'what we do', is primarily an output. In other words, behaviour is the consequence of our thinking processes, either conscious or subconscious, which in their turn may give rise to specific feelings resulting in certain behaviours. We ask you to relate this model to the story below and later develop this model further.

Thinking

Inner Dialogues

Feeling

Behaviour

Outputs

Figure 3.1 Understanding behaviour

> ## Storyboard: 'Beaten before I had begun'
>
> At a meeting, the young executive Martin is waiting to have the oppor-
> tunity to explain his current project in which he has been trying to
> improve distribution by developing a relationship through a third party.
> He has been working on the project for some time and has just made a
> breakthrough that could result in significant profitability. He is now
> anxious to show others the extent of his work.
>
> The meeting deals with a whole range of what appear to be trivial
> issues, and Martin finds himself thinking, 'Why are we talking about
> issues like the new parking arrangements – don't they realize we have
> some much more important matters to discuss?' **(thinking)**
>
> A few minutes later the meeting suddenly seems to change direction
> and starts discussing the need for a new car policy. Martin thinks, 'This
> is ridiculous. I've got far better things to do with my time than sit here
> listening to this rubbish.' **(thinking)**
>
> By now Martin is feeling somewhat irritated and annoyed. **(feelings)**
> These feeling are being demonstrated **(behaviour)** in his looking up at
> the ceiling, sighing deeply and tapping his pen repeatedly on his pad.

In the above example, just forcing Martin to change his behaviour by
stopping him looking at the ceiling or tapping his pen would not have
resulted in a lasting change. Any change that did occur would have tended
to be temporary in nature.

We call this kind of forced change 'white knuckle change', that is to say
a change where we are forcing ourselves to act in a certain way. This forced
behavioural change is contrary to what our thinking dictates. We can bring
about change using this **act as if you are. . .** technique. However, where the
new behaviour dramatically contradicts the pictures we hold in our heads
about ourselves, high levels of stress are often induced, theoretically the
product of dislocation or indeed suppression. Dislocation is a difference
between our emotions and our behaviours, while suppression describes
denial of what we are really feeling.

In order to help Martin, we need to address the way he sees things, his
thinking processes. Only by taking this approach are we likely to achieve
any sort of enduring or lasting change. To do this we might show him how
to re-examine his primary appraisal (how he immediately sees and inter-
prets things) or how to use the alibi technique to change his thinking. A
primary appraisal question you could use with Martin in the above situation
might be 'Is now the best time to do justice to your findings?' Using the alibi
technique you might encourage Martin to develop an alibi for those

discussing parking, for example 'It is important for many people that the parking situation is sorted out. It causes a lot of problems for a lot of people.' Once his thinking has changed, his actions or behaviour will naturally follow: what is more, because the process is not forced, it will be relatively stress-free.

The same can be said of any learning experience. If you truly want to develop your influencing skills, then it is critical that you take the time and spend the necessary energy, developing specific skills or competences like listening or persuasion. However, if such change is to be sustained, then we suggest that you must also consider the need to make sure that your cognitive processes, or the way you see and think about things, are appropriate to what you are seeking to achieve.

Let us now consider in more detail which aspects of our mental processes are of most significance in different business situations.

WE ARE WHAT WE **PERCEIVE**

It is worth pausing here to reflect on how our experiences may have been recorded falsely or in a distorted way. This is a common phenomenon that is concerned primarily with the way our brain makes sense of the world, perception.

Perception is concerned with the way we individually and uniquely interpret the data coming into our brains. The quantity of data is enormous; it is a constant flood of information. We are interpreting from what we see, hear, smell or touch. We will be conscious of some data, while there are other things of which we will be unaware. Given the amount of data, and the speed at which received, it is hardly surprising that sometimes we do not accurately record things as they really are, but as we think they are. Naturally this can cause us problems.

We will return to this subject of perception in the next chapter when we explore ways in which we can tap into the common distortions in human interaction, and how these can be utilized when we influence others. However, let us now consider the impact of cognition on our overall performance. In order to explain these complex processes we use the Model of Performance, Figure 3.2.

This model shows the three key stages we go through when processing data: we start with reflecting on our own behaviour; then through our self-talk we build our self-image; and finally the self-image controls the way we behave. This makes up a cycle of mental events. In other words, we act and behave the way we know or believe we are.

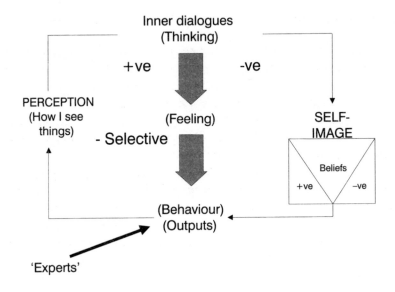

Figure 3.2 The Model of Performance

Let us work through the model from an individual's point of view, taking first of all the frequently adopted pessimistic approach; interestingly, we found that this was an approach taken by many people. We will then look at how the same model fits with a more progressive approach, such as we found in successful individuals. In the next chapter we will explore the techniques which can be practised to develop more powerful mental processes in ourselves.

BEHAVIOUR

Conceptually one could start anywhere in this circle as it reflects a continuous process; however, we will start with the observation 'I engage in behaviour', that is, I do things.

As one of the authors, I am currently sitting at my desk typing this manuscript. I regularly get up to look things up in my reference books or files, and I find myself occasionally looking out of the window into my garden. **I am behaving. As the reader you may be sitting reading this book while relaxing or perhaps travelling or waiting for something or somebody.** You are behaving. The important thing to remember is that we are all behaving all the time. We are always doing something or another; even sitting still is behaviour, albeit passive behaviour.

INNER DIALOGUES

As a result of my behaviour I frequently find myself engaging in inner dialogues; I talk to myself in my head. This is normal; however, often such dialogues assume the nature of background conversations where we find ourselves discussing something with ourselves, almost as if we were two different persons. This is particularly true in conflict situations or where we feel under stress. Generally inner dialogues take place all the time but particularly before and after specific events.

These inner dialogues are based on our perception of reality. As we have seen previously, perception is concerned with the way in which we interpret events. It is notoriously unreliable and prone to distortion, which means that I do not see things necessarily as they are but how I think they are. Consequently these inner dialogues are not necessarily 'the truth', but they are undoubtedly 'our truth'. As a result they are our reality by which we live.

Various studies have shown that many individuals negatively evaluate their own behaviour. We believe that this tendency is probably learnt early on in life primarily from the influence 'experts'.

'Experts'

In addition to what I say to myself about my behaviour, either positive or negative, I am also subjected to another major interpretation of my behaviour which comes from people who have been influential in my life: we call these individuals 'experts'. An 'expert' may be defined as anyone I permit to influence my thinking. Early in my life these people may include my parents, peers, or friends; in later life they may include my spouse, boss, colleagues or indeed anyone who I believe has more experience or knowledge than myself.

The important thing in this notion of 'expert' is that it is only necessary for us to believe that the person has more knowledge than ourselves, rather than that he or she should in fact have such knowledge. As a result it can be seen than many people who are trying to influence others will try to give the idea that they have more knowledge or experience than they do have. In effect, they will try to behave as 'experts'.

Unfortunately for most of us, we have probably had many experiences of 'experts' who have provided a negative rather than a positive influence in our lives. If over time these negative beliefs are reinforced, then we develop a clear picture of who and what we are. Some of these beliefs may be inappropriate; they have their basis not in the truth, but in our (and the other person's) interpretation of the truth. In effect, this is how beliefs are developed.

SELF-IMAGE

Self-image is the sum collection of those attitudes, habits, values and beliefs that are the pictures I hold in my head as to who I am. Self-image acts as a form of control on my behaviour; generally I act in accordance with my self-image, or the way I know or believe that I should act.

In consequence my self-image appears to act as a sort of comfort zone, meaning that when I behave in a way that I know and believe I am, then I am relatively comfortable. When behaving in a way which is inconsistent with my self-image, I am likely to experience a high level of discomfort. Let's think about a social situation to illustrate this point. Perhaps you view yourself as an extrovert: think about behaving as an introvert at a party. How would this make you feel? Perhaps you are an introvert: how would you feel if you started behaving like an extrovert at a party?

To summarize, as individuals we continually interpret our own behaviour using our own perceptual processes but, as we have discussed, these perceptual processes get distorted. If this pattern is repeated, or if we receive corroboration from others whose opinions we value as 'experts', we start to develop beliefs about ourselves. All beliefs have been developed as a result of the processes that we have described above; they are our beliefs, our truths, but are not necessarily 'the' truth. People are not born innately one way or another. No, these beliefs are the result of us repeatedly telling ourselves something positive or negative, or listening to others who also give us positive or negative opinions.

Once a belief starts to take hold, either positively or negatively, our mind continues to conspire against us. This is driven primarily by what we call the LOLO effect. LOLO stands for **lock on, lock out**. It describes the way that once we build a view of the world then our perceptual processes start to **lock on** to things that support our view, while at the same time we **lock out** contrary data or information. This process allows us to perpetuate the belief, ultimately making it more entrenched. Our self-image contains thousands of beliefs. By and large, as long as we act in accordance with these beliefs, or act as we know we should behave, then we stay comfortable, irrespective of whether the beliefs are positive or negative, helpful or handicapping. It is only when we step outside of our self-image that we feel discomfort. Indeed, when this happens we try quickly, often subconsciously, to return to our self-image. In many ways the self-image can be seen as a rudder steering us through life and most of the time we have set the rudder on automatic pilot so it keeps making fine adjustments, often imperceptible, to our overall course.

Let's consider an everyday example of this concept.

Storyboard: 'The 100 man'

Jon was a keen amateur golfer. He had been playing most weeks for over 3 years and despite his numerous lessons, when asked about his performance, he would describe himself as 'a bit of a hacker' or 'the 100 man', making reference to his average score on his local golf course. He almost seemed to pride himself on the predictability of his performance.

On one particular day, Jon was out playing golf with a friend and after completing nine holes he was amazed to find that his score was only 36. He turned and said to his friend, 'It's amazing. I've hit a 36. That's not like me. If I carry on like this, I could come home in about a 72. Amazing!'

He then went on to do his next nine holes. We need not have worried about him hitting a 72 because surprise, surprise, he did the next nine in 65 coming in at 101.

This example shows how self-defeating beliefs about performance can be. Of course Jon desperately wanted to hit a score of 72, but he had such a strong belief structure telling him he was 'the 100 man' that it was hard to work against it!

POSITIVE **THINKING**

So self-image controls our behaviour. But what about positive thinking? You may have heard of catch-phrases such as 'the power of positive thinking' or 'think positive'. This idea has been around for many years. In some respects it is somewhat simplistic, yet it does provide us with a useful way of exploring the importance of positive mental attitude.

In our research we asked some of the most successful chief executive officers and senior managers of major international organizations to explain the approaches they use to help build their own confidence and ensure that, in business situations, they are likely to be successful. Examples of their objectives included:

- achieving desired results in meetings;
- influencing other people;
- removing worries of not being able to cope;
- overcoming fears of using personal computers;
- improving personal abilities in high profile presentations.

What our research revealed was that there are apparently some commonly used psychological techniques and methods that appear to be used quite naturally by these successful managers, and the use of these techniques seemed to contribute significantly to their success.

You may be thinking, 'Surely the top chief executive officers and senior managers cannot all use the same methods and approaches.' Certainly we would agree, but what we did identify were a few common approaches which managers use either consciously or subconsciously in their normal working lives. We have observed particularly that a common characteristic of all these successful individuals is their tendency to use positive thinking as well as visualization of success.

We also found that by introducing these techniques on skills development and management development programmes, managers significantly increase their chances of success and are more likely to develop skills resulting in lasting changes in behaviour. The skills of using imagery are described later in this chapter, and methods for challenging and changing our self-image are discussed in the last chapter.

You might like to consider at this stage some of your own personal goals. These could be related to influencing, for example:

- to improve ability in persuading senior management;
- to develop skills in giving feedback to others;
- to improve assertiveness in conflict situations;
- to stay controlled in difficult situations;
- to make a good first impression on other people.

The examples quoted above are expressed in quite broad terms. What we do suggest is that you turn your general aims into more specific targets, and more importantly consider how you can make sure that you achieve them. The technique of positive thinking combined with the use of visualization can be very useful in helping you achieve your aims. Let us now explore the practical use of these techniques.

USING **VISUALIZATION**

The Model of Performance, discussed earlier in the chapter, may seem rather pessimistic. There is, though, a much more optimistic possibility. Working against the tendency toward negative inner dialogues, by use of techniques that encourage positive image, can break the vicious circle. The use of such ideas can help you develop a positive self-image resulting in effective behavioural change and more successful influencing.

The two specific techniques covered here are those of drafting 'self-assertion statements' and the use of visualization as a way of successfully imprinting positive images as new beliefs. These techniques have been born out of our original research into the common characteristics displayed by highly successful individuals, as well as successful influencers in organizations, and are backed up by earlier findings about methods used by successful sportsmen and sportswomen.

But first, let's consider the story of an aspiring entrepreneur, which is based on a discussion we had with a successful businessman regarding the way he achieved his success.

Storyboard: The aspiring entrepreneur

When starting my own business, I did not really see myself as an entrepreneur; indeed, I did not really know how business people became aware of business opportunities. Essentially I had a picture of myself as a corporate manager within a big blue-chip company. We were always the buyers of services and I saw myself as a good buyer – after all, I had plenty of experience of sitting back whilst the salespeople flocked to see me. I then decided who to do business with.

Shortly after starting my own business it became glaringly obvious that entrepreneurial skills were going to be integral to the success of the venture. The clients were not going to simply come knocking on my door. I had a choice: either I committed myself to becoming 'gamekeeper turned poacher' or I employed someone with strong sales skills. I knew the problem on an intellectual level but that didn't seem to help me when it came to changing my behaviour or doing anything different.

As it turned out, the problem was not so much my actual ability to generate business, but more to do with my self-concept and the messages I had given myself over the years. As a result, I committed to spend a few minutes each day trying to imagine myself seeing and developing business opportunities.

As a result of this type of thinking process, something strange seemed to happen: I started to see a number of different opportunities. In particular, I remember one specific event that was to change the way I would see myself for ever.

One evening in the early days of the new business, I was sitting enjoying a meal in a public restaurant with my family when I found myself overhearing a conversation between two businessmen. As their discussion developed, I recognized the situation they were describing,

---

> and it struck me that their problem was my business opportunity. I found myself visualizing their particular organization and, equally importantly, could see myself actually approaching them in order to explore opportunities for doing business with them. My business card was in their hands before they had finished their coffee; and by then they had agreed to meet with me the following week.
>
> Fortunately that contact not only generated some valuable early business but also, as a result of repeatedly going over it in my mind (**imprinting**) and talking to others, it had a profound effect on how I viewed myself.
>
> From that time on I started to see business opportunities; and, equally importantly, my new belief about myself allowed me to follow up such opportunities. Hardly a day would pass without me identifying at least one chance to demonstrate my newly acquired entrepreneurial flair.

The above anecdote is drawn from a semi-structured interview with someone who was identified as a successful influencer by colleagues. It demonstrates in a less theoretical way the real power of the self-image and how we act in accordance with the pictures that we have of ourselves, which may be self-limiting. It also shows the way positive imprinting and repetition can bring about changes in the self-image that ultimately lead to significant improvements in performance.

The entrepreneur describes three important issues. First, there is the ability to use visualization as a way of seeing specific opportunities for succeeding in a new job role or skill. Insight into our own behaviour in itself is insufficient; it was the use of imagery that galvanized the latent entrepreneur into action. Second, our ability to visualize or picture success is something more than simply 'positive thinking'. If we can manage the pictures we carry in our heads of ourselves or of situations, and if we can recognize and develop the internal conversations we have, then our heightened perception will result in us achieving the things that we want. In short, 'seeing' things is the prerequisite to taking action. Third, we are moved into action by the repeated use of this imagery, and more repetition produces lasting and sustained change.

To demonstrate the power of these principles, try the following simple experiment. The next time you are driving into your local town and are worried that you will not be able to find a parking space, instead of waiting till you arrive in the town centre and then getting into a cycle of negative self-talk about the lack of parking spaces, spend time as you are driving thinking along the following lines:

1. Try to visualize the town centre, particularly the area that you would like to park in. Try to see as much detail as possible.
2. Picture where the cars are usually parked.
3. Imagine yourself reversing into a space somewhere in the general area.
4. Imagine your feeling of relief at finding a place so soon.

As a result of undertaking the above you may be surprised at how quickly you find a parking space. This is caused primarily as a result of your perception being heightened; you see things that were always there; you start seeing the numerous parking opportunities you previously convinced yourself did not exist. In short, as a result of this technique you will find that when you get to within 800 metres of where you have been visualizing, you will suddenly start seeing all the opportunities for parking like:

- people reaching in their pockets for their car keys;
- exhaust pipes starting up;
- doors opening;
- people walking determinedly towards vehicles.

With this technique you are visualizing success and utilizing the way in which perception works; you lock onto the opportunities that abound. Of course the more traditional approach would be to wait until you have arrived at where you want to be, and then be surprised at not seeing opportunities. By the time you arrive, you have already missed all the major opportunities. In this negative example, life has passed us by!

More specifically, successful influencers appear to possess strong imaginative skills, including the ability to picture or visualize situations. What they also do is channel these skills into visualizing success in influencing situations. We believe that the use of visualization and imagery are skills that can be developed and refined.

Exercise: practising imagination

Consider the following exercise that explores your basic skills of imagery:

1. Close your eyes and relax.

2. Imagine you are lying asleep in bed at home. You wake up and it is very quiet and still dark outside. Your throat is very dry and after realizing that you are not going to fall back to sleep you decide to go and get a drink.
3. You get out of bed and because of your familiarity with your home you make your way to the kitchen without putting on any of the lights. Standing in front of the refrigerator you pull the door open and the light makes you blink.
4. Looking inside the refrigerator you see a lemon on the top shelf. You reach for the lemon; it feels cold and waxy in your hand. You take it out of the refrigerator and shut the door. Once again it is dark.
5. You open a drawer where you know you will find a knife and using the breadboard you cut the lemon in half. You reach towards one half of the lemon and move it towards your mouth. You bite hard. . .

Consider the following:

- Did you salivate?
- Could you actually taste the lemon?
- Did you feel the waxy cold skin of the lemon?
- On a scale of 0 (low)–10(high) what level of detail in the house were you able to see?

Successful people we interviewed scored highly in this exercise in terms of their ability to visualize the above scene as though it were real; they described experiencing the sensations of temperature, taste and sound and being able to see the scene in a vivid way. In particular they tended to rate the final question as seven or above.

The interesting thing in this specific exercise is that it recognizes that when we use imagery and visualization, we do not only see pictures, but also hear, smell, taste and touch. Along with these sensations you may experience emotions or moods. Indeed, in developing our imagery skills we should always try to incorporate as many of the senses as possible. Let us move on to use the same skills of visualization but this time in a real situation.

Exercise: real visualization

1. To start, think of an influencing situation that you are about to undertake.
2. Sit comfortably and try to relax, maybe closing your eyes, and take in a few deep breaths, exhaling slowly.

3. Now think of the situation and the person involved in detail. Try to see him or her in your imagination.
   - What does the place look like?
   - What might you or the other person be wearing?
   - How would the other person greet you?
   - Who else would be there?
   - Would you be standing or sitting?
4. Next visualize what you might say to the other person. See him or her responding positively to you, maybe laughing, nodding or saying yes.
5. Finally, using your imagination, try to see as much detail as you can.

Hold the image as long as you can. If possible, feel the emotions that would accompany the successful outcome.

Remember: Visualize only success!

To increase the likelihood of achieving your personal goals you will almost certainly need to address these internal issues as well as acquiring the external, skill-based competences and techniques. It is commonly accepted that one way of developing effective behaviour and learning is to use mental rehearsal or imagery. Since the 1950s we have known that mental performance improves physical performance. Indeed, there is hardly a biography written today where the individual does not proclaim the virtues of mental practice as a way of improving physical performance.

As previously described, our own research suggests that successful individuals engage in similar processes before specific events. So for example, before giving a presentation an individual may take a minute to sit back and try to visualize a successful outcome. This could include seeing smiling faces, seeing others nodding their heads or even hearing the sound of hands clapping. There is evidence to suggest that in these circumstances it is desirable to imagine as much detail as possible, as it appears that the greater the level of detail, the higher the levels of imprinting onto our minds. In a similar way repetition may be a useful technique to employ. You are now given the opportunity to reflect using the following questions.

PAUSE FOR **THOUGHT**

1. *How much of your self-talk is positive?*
2. *What beliefs do you hold about your influencing skills?*
3. *Are these beliefs helpful or a hindrance?*

4. *Where or how did you get these beliefs?*
5. *Are these beliefs real (do you have hard evidence?) or to what extent are they a result of distorted perception?*
6. *Have you ever been aware of how your thinking processes gave rise to behaviour and how, when you changed your thoughts, that behaviour changed automatically? What caused the change of thinking?*
7. *Try and identify some occasion that you actively used positive thinking to help you with a difficult or important situation. What were the circumstances? Did you get what you wanted?*

SELF-FULFILLING **PROPHECY**

The concept of the self-fulfilling prophecy is especially relevant to situations where we are attempting to influence others; indeed, the use of imagery and visualization in itself can be self-fulfilling. In simplistic terms, self-fulfilling prophecy is about how expectations, of ourselves or of others, influence outcome.

The phenomenon of the self-fulfilling prophecy was identified by psychological experiments that were carried out on a class of school children. Psychologists categorized the class into intelligent children, likely to perform well, and less intelligent children, more likely to fail. The categorization was random, and not based on any assessment as to which children were intelligent and which were not. The teacher was not informed that this was an experiment but was given the supposed result of the 'tests'. The psychologists returned a year later to study end-of-year results. It was discovered that those categorized as intelligent had succeeded whereas those categorized as less intelligent had been less successful.

It was then revealed that the split into two categories had been a random one. The research found that the expectations of the teacher translated into actions and attitudes, and affected the way the pupils were treated; this in turn affected the behaviour of the pupils. Clearly the ethics of such an experiment are debatable; however, the concept of self-fulfilling prophecy, something we commonly recognize, was proved.

The term 'self-fulfilling prophecy' is used to describe the way that we can influence the performance and behaviour of others simply through the way we deal with them and through our expectations: the prophecy becomes self-fulfilling. Further research revealed this phenomenon in a number of other areas including in the organizational world.

The self-fulfilling prophecy concept frequently has negative connotations. Consider the impact parents have on their children by using phrases such as 'She's not too academic' or 'He is the world's most untidy child', and how after hearing this many times the child then incorporates this as a self-belief and acts in accordance with it. This contributes to the formation of self-image.

The upside of the self-fulfilling prophecy is that it can work in a positive way. Many of the successful people we interviewed in our research suggested that their success was driven by a strong positive belief held about them by others, perhaps a sports coach, parent or senior manager. Interestingly some also described how they had been able to channel some of the negative beliefs held by others into achieving positive outcomes in order to disprove the negative views. One memorable example of this came from one of the highest paid chief executives in Europe during the economic boom of the 1980s, who said he was driven primarily by overhearing a conversation which his parents were having with friends. He heard his mother say, 'Oh, Rolf will never achieve much. He's a lovely lad but it's his sister who has all the brains and concentration.'

In the context of attempting to influence others we should consider what sort of expectations we have of them and the extent to which we demonstrate these expectations. If we try to influence team members to develop certain skills or attitudes, but we believe they are unlikely to achieve them, then we should not be surprised when they fail. A useful approach if we are operating in such a dynamic is to use positive terminology and to create strong pictures of what success looks like rather than dwelling on the existing negatives. For example, when setting the target, discuss and describe what success will look like. Too often the reverse happens and, as team leaders, we describe the obstacles and pitfalls to watch out for, thus highlighting the negative.

PAUSE FOR **THOUGHT**

1. *Think about a discussion you are having with team members. Are you highlighting the obstacles or describing what success looks like?*
2. *What preconceived ideas do you hold about team members?*
3. *How are these ideas affecting performance?*

In this chapter we have begun looking at the importance of cognition on performance. Indeed, the principles that we have been examining can be useful in helping us improve our influencing skills, and they also have a broader application towards our ongoing development. In particular we have focused on the use of positive thought and visualization as ways of increasing the likelihood of success in an influencing situation. In Chapter 9, we will continue with some of these principles and extend them into your ongoing development as an influencer. We now explore the pleasantries and preface stage of the influencing process, focusing on the competences of impact and rapport.

four

PLEASANTRIES AND
PREFACE

At the completion of this chapter the reader will:

- understand what good impact and rapport are in an influencing situation;
- have considered how impact can be managed best, having explored the most common reasons why people fail to make a positive impact;
- know the importance of building rapport, and be able to describe a four-step model of how relationships develop and the stages through which relationships decline;
- be able to state the importance of preface and describe ways in which we gain interest from those who are uninterested.

INTRODUCTION

Pleasantries are about how we gain effective entry to the influencing process; if the pleasantries and preface stage is managed effectively, then it is more likely that the opportunities for influencing at a later stage will be increased. By contrast, there is evidence to suggest that if this step of entry is mismanaged then the chances of success are considerably reduced.

In the previous chapters, we explored various aspects of preparation that are normally the prerequisite to effective influencing. In this chapter, the key competences for effective pleasantries are impact and building rapport; while in preface the key competences are arousal and maintaining interest. As can be seen in our choice of title for this book, we consider impact to be critical when influencing. We explore impressions and impact, themes that we develop further in subsequent chapters, and then we explore how you can develop relationships that facilitate influencing.

This chapter first explores impressions management and how to develop the right impression. We move on to how you can develop rapport and trust in relationships as a foundation for influencing. We then look at how you can create arousal and maintain interest in an influencing encounter.

INTRODUCING IMPRESSION AND **IMPACT**

The ability to make an immediate impact and a positive impression on the person or group you are intending to influence is absolutely critical to success. Consider the implications of some of the research into first impressions. This research suggests that people form 90 per cent of their opinion of another person in the first 90 seconds of an encounter (Pease, 1984). We see this in the recruitment interview where interviewers often describe having a 'gut feel' about the candidate right from the start of the interview. In general the importance of making impact right at the start of any meeting cannot be overestimated.

We often hear expressions such as 'first impressions count', 'make a good impression' and 'you do not get a second chance to make a first impression'. In a similar vein there are some interesting connotations associated with impressions such as 'all that glitters is not gold', 'a wolf in sheep's clothing' and 'do not judge a book by its cover'. Implicit in these sayings is the possibility of being deceived by first impressions. We will refer to this concept of managing the impressions which others form of us as 'impressions management'. Throughout the book we will look at several ways in which someone's perception of his or her reality can be distorted, and how knowledge and judicious application of techniques can help increase the power of personal influence.

First impressions are an aspect of impressions management on which it is possible to capitalize positively. Other people's perceptions of us can be skewed, which allows us to encourage them to see us in a different way. Such an approach, it has been suggested, capitalizes on the 'distortion' of first impressions. It is not our intention to support a deceptive strategy; but, like it or not, when we meet others for the first time they form a first impression of us, falling in the range of good to poor. Impressions management is about ensuring that we give ourselves the best possible chance of giving the right impression.

The competence we call rapport follows naturally from that of impact and is essentially about building trust quickly so that the other person feels that a strong relationship exists and that there is some bond between the two parties. Some people are naturally strong in their ability to do this whereas others find this the most difficult aspect of influencing. Rapport needs to be established in the early part of the relationship and then reinforced continually throughout. We will be looking at some of the techniques which effective influencers use in order to build rapport.

Cultural differences are again an important consideration when attempting to make an impact and create rapport. As with the competence of preparation we will look at some of the researched cultural differences which have implications for how we might adjust our approach to making impact and building rapport when doing business with people from different cultural backgrounds.

BUILDING THE RIGHT **IMPRESSION**

Why is it that some people make impact when they simply enter the room? Others say about these rare people, 'He just has charisma' or 'I cannot explain why but other people just sit up and listen to her'. Often people talk about these qualities as though they are genetic; you either have it or you do not. It has previously been considered that these charismatic traits, often associated with successful leaders, are natural rather than learnt. We will not be debating here the classic argument of whether our personality is determined before we are born or shaped by subsequent learning. Suffice to say we strongly believe the ability to make impact is something that can be developed and improved through understanding and practice.

To make an impact there are a number of things you can do. Equally there are a number of things you should definitely not do. In a sense these are the more straightforward techniques to understand and practise. Then there are the things you possibly or probably should or should not do, depending on circumstances. These are really dependent on the style and cultural background of the person you are trying to influence and this is where a degree of judgement and a good deal of common sense are called for.

PROMOTE YOURSELF

Frequently in British culture one hears children being told not to 'show off'; there is a cultural norm which says that talking about your own successes is immodest and could be seen as arrogant. Even if someone else compliments you on an achievement or strength you are expected to respond in a suitably humble manner. In some cultures and societies the roots of such behaviours and norms can be traced back through history. This is borne out by the following statement from the Victorian Mrs Humphry in *Manners For Men*, who wrote in 1897, 'The truth is that society demands a never-ending series of self-denying actions from those who belong to it, and the more cheerfully these are performed, the more perfect the manners' (Jessop, 1994). In a similar way Mark Twain said, 'Good breeding consists of concealing how much we think of ourselves and how little we think of the other person.'

For children who are socialized heavily in this way some similar behaviours are transferred into adulthood. This is often the reason why we hear people respond to praise in the following ways:

- 'Oh, it's nothing really.'
- 'Thanks, but I was just lucky.'
- 'Actually, I'm not that good.'
- 'It wasn't all to do with me – I had a lot of help.'

Contrast this with the approach taken by one US multinational consumer-goods giant, which has built official bragging into its performance management system. If you feel you have achieved something out of the ordinary you are encouraged to complete a 'brag sheet', which is submitted to your manager. If it is felt that the achievement is sufficiently notable, he or she will send it to the head office in the United States. But the system does not stop there; if the senior managers are suitably impressed they will send the brag sheet back with a written note of praise.

Those who are successful in terms of making impact do not feel guilty about letting others know about their successes. They will be their own best public relations agents. Clearly, if it is possible to have someone else sing your praises to a third party, then this will prove to be an even more powerful way of making impact. This is the reason that a junior colleague will often accompany a senior manager on a business meeting. The junior can be suitably in awe of the omniscient senior manager. Similarly if you are making a high profile presentation, try to arrange for someone to introduce you officially, and brief him or her about your achievements and successes so as to ensure a strong introduction.

In informal discussion, do not be afraid to promote yourself. This could mean talking about a recent project with which you are pleased. If this is done in a suitable tone without being overbearing then it need not seem too egocentric and opinionated; if you sound confidently surprised and pleased with your achievements, your enthusiasm is likely to spread. And to ensure you are seen to be entirely reasonable and balanced, talk about the success which the other person has had; this will help with building rapport.

An important point on making impact and building rapport is to remember to build your personal credibility slowly. This means that, rather than letting everything about yourself be known on first meeting, you should let additional things be known slowly; this is done best in an oblique manner, through half-references or innuendo.

CHOOSE YOUR WORDS WITH CARE

The words you choose when attempting to make impact are very important and it is worth considering the effect that certain words are likely to have on others, rather than relying simply on your own interpretation. Some words are likely to make others sit up and listen from the start. This has to be a key consideration for the entry stage of the influencing process. Other words, although of similar meaning, may be less likely to gain attention. The words that make impact are sometimes referred to as 'power words'. A list of power words and phrases, and broadly equivalent 'weaker words', is shown in Table 4.1.

In a similar way there are some words which have emotive connotations for the person hearing them despite the fact that they are used without

Table 4.1 Power words and weaker words

Power words/expressions	Weaker words/expressions
Definitely	Possibly
Clearly	Maybe
The only option	Perhaps we . . .
Leading edge	New
Pioneering	New
The new technology is . . .	The latest thing is . . .
Giant	Big
Achieved	Did
Specifically	What I mean is . . .
Renowned	Well known
Success	Good thing
Power of	Use of
Impact	Significance
Immediately	As soon as possible

the intention of stirring such emotion. A good example of this is the word 'but'. This commonly used word can be interpreted as blocking and negative, whereas the words 'however' and 'and' hold similar meanings but without such potential for negative interpretation. When you hear yourself about to say 'but', try to use 'however' or 'and' which convey a more supportive approach.

Similarly the use, early in a discussion, of the word 'problem', particularly if couched in terms such as 'your problem' or 'the problem you have is. . .', can seem quite accusatory and threatening. The use of the word 'issue' may achieve the same purpose in a less threatening way, for example 'The issue we need to address is. . .'. Notice here the use of 'we' rather than 'you'; again this is less confrontational and may help in setting the appropriate tone early on in the discussion.

GET NOTICED

We are not proposing here that it is necessary to dress up or act so as to appear different, but in order to make impact at the start it does help to look distinctive. This could be demonstrated through subtle detail such as interesting cufflinks, buckles or brooches, or even a distinctive fountain pen. Some people have made certain characteristics their trade mark, say unusual ties or brightly coloured handkerchiefs; the danger is that the feature, if it appears as a gimmick, may become more of a focus of interest than the person or message.

Undoubtedly an important consideration about dress and appearance is to have some understanding of the cultural norms for the organization, profession or nationality of the people you are attempting to influence. While it may not be sensible to mimic the dress conventions of the other parties, it may prove helpful to modify or adjust your appearance in order to show some identification with them. If consulting with a client organization in a UK government department in London, anything other than dark or formal clothing may seem revolutionary. The expectation may be that in order to continue to work with this organization conformity is essential; this means that any attempt to be noticed will need to be discreet and subtle. Conversely it is possible to visit a creative advertising agency in the same street where it will be expected that one should wear bright colours and informal clothing. In this environment the dark suit, which would have been entirely appropriate for the government department, will be viewed as staid and unimaginative. The corollary of this is the assumption that the person too lacks imagination and creativity, qualities which are considered important in this sort of organization.

Many successful influencers we have interviewed have described the importance of being able to demonstrate chameleon-like qualities, in other words the ability to adjust one's appearance and style according to the people or group one is attempting to influence. The trick is be able to strike a balance between blending in with the environment and retaining some distinctive and memorable qualities or features.

SPEAK UP

In group discussion situations it has been found that those who speak first tend to be viewed by others as influential. It is the early intervention that makes a major impact even though the more reserved members of the group may have more to contribute. It is vital to speak up from the start, though this sometimes can prove difficult.

If you are unsure what to say or fear that you may make a fool of yourself by saying the wrong thing, then simply try stating the objective of the discussion, or building on and adding to the comments of another early speaker. Frequently the difficulty when making an early contribution is finding an opportunity to 'get in'. This is because more forceful characters tend to dominate. There are some interesting lessons to be drawn from these more dominant people. How is it that they manage to have their say early on and others seem to listen? Some interesting techniques are:

■ speaking but avoiding eye contact with other people, thereby making it more difficult for others to signal non-verbally that they want to interrupt. This takes a degree of confidence and it is necessary to suggest through a deliberate tone of voice that you are not going to stop;
■ prefacing the input with a 'trailer' which raises awareness and interest in what is to follow, for instance comments such as, 'And do you know why this is important? I'll tell you why. . .' or 'Here is the real issue. . .'. This draws attention and raises the expectation that there is more to come;
■ agreeing with another person and adding to his or her comments but 'adding value' to them from your own experience. An example of this would be a comment such as, 'Of course you are right, Michelle – in fact I have found the same problem. The approach I took was. . .';
■ raising the volume of the voice, an obvious but frequently neglected technique. Some people have voices that carry naturally, whereas for others it is more difficult physically to speak up;

■ grabbing attention by raising the volume and then deliberately lowering it so that the listeners, having become interested, have to work to hear the more quiet contribution. This is an effective technique. It is as though the quieter voice, contrasting with the early contribution, suggests a conspiratorial or secret discussion, which others will not want to miss out on.

The early part of a discussion is often found to be difficult when communicating with people of a different culture from our own. This is due to the existence of strong cultural norms of which we may not be aware. Even if we are, we tend to work from our own cultural frame of reference. In an Anglo-Saxon culture, for example, it is normal for one person to speak, complete the input and then for the other person to start speaking. In a Latin culture, by contrast, it is more common for the inputs to overlap. In an Oriental culture, however, silences between inputs are common. It should not come as a surprise, given these cultural norms, that a German plunged into a meeting with a group of Italians feels uncomfortable because of the difficulty experienced when trying to gain an entry. The German will be waiting for an appropriate opportunity to make a contribution, whereas the Italians are likely to operate in a much more interactive way with perhaps four or five people talking at once. The opportunity for a formal input may never come. It is a question of recognizing the cultural difference and working with it rather than fighting it.

Of course these cultural differences work both ways and if one of the Italians was invited back to the German's organization, the same difficulties could be experienced but on this occasion with the Italian feeling uncomfortable with the formality of structured inputs at predetermined times.

USE POWERFUL BODY LANGUAGE

Body language, the non-verbal cues and signals we give out, sometimes consciously, often unconsciously, is incredibly powerful in terms of impact, which is why we devote Chapter 7 to the subject. At the early stage of an interaction it is critical to portray positive body language. Other people are likely to work on our body language for interpretation and meaning, even more than on the words spoken. Examples of positive and negative body language are given below.

Clearly it is simplistic to suggest that these positive examples of body language taken in isolation will always be interpreted in a positive way. It is more likely that the person on whom you are attempting to make an impact

Table 4.2 Body language

Positive body language	Negative body language
Smiling when appropriate	Grinning (may be seen as patronizing)
	Scowling (may be seen as aggressive)
Shaking hands or bowing confidently	Hesitant handshake (may be interpreted as weakness)
Sitting or standing upright	Slouching back (may be seen as disinterest)
Varied intonation – use of range of tones	Monotone voice (may be interpreted as uninterest on the part of the speaker or indicate the subject is boring)
	Quiet, low voice (may be seen as uncertainty or lack of confidence)
Making eye contact	Staring (may seem intrusive)
	Looking away (may be viewed as disinterest or viewed with suspicion)
Open gestures such as facing the other person and raising eyebrows	Crossing legs and arms (may be viewed as defensive)
Upright or slightly tilted head to show listening	Bowed head (may be seen as shyness or nervousness)

will look to a number of sources or 'clusters' of non-verbal behaviour for the real message. In this way he or she will piece together evidence from sources such as facial expressions, sitting position, gestures and tone of voice. When you are trying to make impact consider whether the non-verbal signals you are giving are consistent with the verbal message and whether they are likely to enhance or diminish your profile. Perhaps you could ask trusted friends or colleagues for their views on this question. As stated, we will be exploring body language in more detail in Chapter 7.

SEE THE SIGNALS

The danger with focusing on making a major impact at the start of the influencing process is that we overemphasize the importance of portraying messages to others at the expense of reading the signals which they themselves, either overtly or inadvertently, are giving out. It can be very informative to look for the non-verbal messages and consider how to adapt accordingly. For instance:

■ **Are they looking anxious?**
  It may be necessary to spend more time putting them at ease or making 'small talk' or it may help to try to identify the source of the anxiety.

■ **Do they seem preoccupied?**
  It may help to try and find out the real issues that they would like to discuss rather than just the stated objective.

■ **Are they giving out hostile signals?**
  If you know the source of the hostility it may help to bring this discussion out into the open, or if you are uncertain of the source, some gentle probing may identify their perception of the problem.

■ **Do they look uninterested?**
  It could be that you need to raise their interest by relating the subject to them personally or you may need to make a high impact statement such as 'Do you realize some of your colleagues have doubled their salary in the last year by focusing on this issue?'

It is always worth paying close attention to the actual words and terminology used by other people. Often this means looking for subtleties or 'neon signs', signals that people give us, which prompt us to ask additional questions. Consider, for instance, issues in their organization: do they talk about departments, units, sections or divisions? Do they distinguish their territory by regions, districts or areas? Are there certain words or expressions that you can identify as taboo? For example, managers in an organization may prefer to talk about development reviews rather than performance appraisals. The two expressions could be used to refer to the same process but the organization may have a history of a failed 'performance appraisal' scheme. Pick up the language used by the other person, then try to echo back the same words when presenting your own points of view. This may mean working from the other person's frame of reference rather than purely from your own, but it will certainly help in encouraging him or her to identify with you.

LESSENING **IMPACT**

Just as there are a number of techniques you can deploy in attempting to make a positive impact, there are also a number of 'impact killers' to be aware of. These are mistakes that are often made without even knowing it. Examples of impact killers are:

Self-deprecating comments

These are comments, often used to preface a statement, which lower the status of the speaker. Often self-deprecating comments are meant to demonstrate modesty but they do little more than weaken the impact of the statement which follows.

Examples of self-deprecating statements are, 'I don't really know much about this but what I think we should do is. . .' or 'I am certainly no expert in this field but why don't we consider. . .'. In contrast to this approach our studies of successful influencers have shown that such people will be very cautious about putting themselves down publicly. This does not mean covering up weaknesses and attempting to portray omniscience, but it does mean showing respect for one's own views and opinions, and not sharing negative inner dialogues with others.

Compromising on quality

If you compromise on quality, the chances are it will show. This is about taking short cuts or ignoring mistakes. An example of compromising on quality would be making a presentation with well-prepared slides but allowing one or two slides with spelling mistakes to be used rather than correcting them; or it could be demonstrated by the acceptance of low standards in others which might be shown through comments such as 'Oh, that will do' or 'This will be good enough.'

Mispronouncing or misspelling names

This can be a tricky matter particularly when working in an international environment, but mispronouncing the name of the person you are attempting to influence is one certain way of making a negative impact. You may be lucky and find the other person is forgiving or understanding because he or she recognizes that the name can be mispronounced easily. You will gain more credibility, however, by checking you have pronounced the name correctly, or asking how it should be pronounced, and making a point of getting it right. It is a dangerous strategy to guess.

Not being well informed

Being ill informed is another certain impact killer. This could mean having out-of-date information or not knowing about important changes in the other person's circumstances or organization. Conversely actually demonstrating you are well informed and up to date will help in establishing impact. It is not always possible to have the latest information or insider knowledge and if you are aware there may be some news of which you are uninformed, then exercise some caution when demonstrating your knowledge. If you are uncertain of facts and figures that you are expected to have to hand, it can be a mistake to try to bluff. A much better tactic is to promise to seek out the information and provide it at a later date. You will gain more credibility by honouring your commitment than by trying to suggest you have knowledge when you do not.

Allowing repeated interruptions

The final main impact killer is allowing constant interruptions. Some people have a tendency to allow others to interrupt them repeatedly. While allowing the occasional interruption may demonstrate an ability to listen to the other person, allowing repeated interruptions will eventually be interpreted as a lack of self-esteem, which will clearly reduce impact when influencing.

PAUSE FOR **THOUGHT**

1. *Think of someone who made an immediate positive impact upon you. What was it specifically he or she did or said which contributed to this impact? What were the non-verbal messages conveyed?*
2. *Now consider someone to whom you took an instant dislike. What was it specifically he or she said or did which contributed to this dislike? What was it, if anything, about his or her appearance that you disliked?*
3. *What assumptions were you making about these people based on first impressions? If you got to know them better, how well founded were your assumptions?*

We have considered a number of ways of making impact, some of which, to be effective, should be demonstrated early on in the interaction. That is not to say the techniques of making impact do not apply throughout the influencing process, but it is the first four minutes which really count in terms of making a powerful first impression.

We now highlight a cultural difference of note. In a Japanese culture the ritual of the first meeting includes an overt display of respect for the ascribed status of the two parties. The ritual demands that the two people hold their business cards out in front of them and, together, bow deferentially and exchange cards. The cards are then studied for some time while each party respectfully notes the job title and level of the other person.

You need to be aware of cultural differences. As it is impractical to list all these differences here, we urge you to research them before engaging in any influencing situation so as to help you make the right first impression.

We will now look at the competence of building rapport which follows on from making impact.

LAYING THE FOUNDATIONS: BUILDING **RAPPORT**

Rapport is about building trust or laying the foundations of a relationship and consequently enabling the other person to feel that you have something in common with him or her. There are some specific techniques for building rapport used by powerful influencers, which can be defined and practised. Before we look at the techniques it will be helpful to discuss a model that looks at how relationships are formed and strengthened.

HOW RELATIONSHIPS DEVELOP

If the ability to build rapport is about being able to accelerate the development of a human relationship, then it is helpful to look at the process by which relationships are built.

The model in Figure 4.1 illustrates an interesting example of how the psychologists who developed it used one particular influencing technique to great effect. While the name of the model 'Johari window' suggests

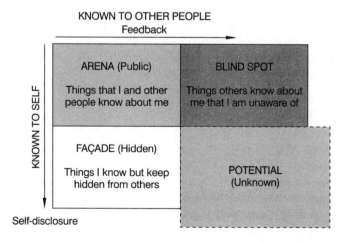

Figure 4.1 Developing relationships with others

some complex and even mystical meaning and source, it is actually a combination of the first names, Jo and Harry, of the two psychologists who created it. While this is quite amusing, there is a message here about influencing. This method of establishing expertise by using technical or pseudo-technical language can be a very effective persuasive technique for establishing credibility.

The Johari window model uses the concept of windows to show how we tend to relate to other people around us. According to the model, there are four windows which exist in our relationships with others. The horizontal axis shown on the top of the windows refers to what is known by others about us. The vertical axis shown to the left of the windows refers to information known by us about ourselves. Each window represents a certain amount of information about us.

So the arena represents all that information about me which is known by myself and others; this is where we operate. When we first meet another person, the arena tends to consist of psychologically safe information, which is invariably of a factual nature. This includes information such as names, job roles, locations, nationalities and other personal, but not too personal, information.

Then there are the things in the top right window that are known by others about me but of which I am unaware. You may be wondering how others can have personal knowledge that I do not possess about myself. Surely I am the authority on myself. Well possibly, but this window is referred to as the blind spot because it contains a lot of information about, for instance, mannerisms, habits and behaviours of which others are more conscious. The only way to increase our consciousness of these factors is through a process of feedback, be it requested or imposed.

The lower left window represents the hidden or facade. This is the window concealing a lot of personal information which, in most superficial relationships, we tend to keep hidden. This could include information about our personal tastes, beliefs, religious views, upbringing, childhood, personal relationships and weaknesses. This sort of information may remain concealed from all but a handful of people; those who are aware of what lies behind the facade are likely to be those who are nearest and dearest to us. We may, however, expose different parts of this window to different individuals.

Finally, there is the lower right window, which represents our potential; this contains information that we ourselves do not know necessarily and of which others are unaware. Our potential is what we could achieve, if, conceptually, we were able to reduce the blind spot and façade. This is the crux of the model: in order to reduce the blind spot we need to seek feedback and in order to reduce the façade we need to reveal more information to others so that they have a better understanding of why we are the way we are. This can seem quite threatening because, if we receive feedback, we may not like what we hear and if we disclose personal information then others may not like what they hear. In some cultures, such as in the Middle East, self-disclosure is frowned upon because it may mean exposing weaknesses, and there is an underlying fear that others could use this information in the future to their advantage and to one's own disadvantage. The Johari window is a model of how relationships develop because as we become closer to certain individuals, whether family, friends or partners, there is a tendency to disclose more information and to give and receive more honest feedback.

Now let's consider ways of building rapport with those we are attempting to influence. Those who are particularly effective in their ability to develop rapport in a short time tend to use certain techniques in order to establish trust and create the impression that there is a bond or relationship between the two parties. Critical in this rapport-building process is the very early part of the relationship or discussion. This is not to say that rapport building takes place and is then forgotten; strong influencers will continue to build rapport throughout the discussion and will refer back to some of the subject matter discussed early on as a way of continuing to move closer to the other person.

The primary time for starting to build rapport is, as with impact, within the first four minutes. This is the stage when both parties, irrespective of status and experience, are likely to feel apprehensive about how the relationship is going to evolve. If there is little or no knowledge of the other person, then normally the very early part of the interaction will be marked with formality and caution as each person attempts to weigh up the other.

USING SMALL TALK

The most effective rapport builders will invest time at this stage trying to break the ice, often through conversation that may seem trivial in relation to the real agenda, and which conforms to the safe arena of the Johari window. This level of conversation may be referred to as 'small talk'. In the UK, small talk tends to revolve around the weather; at an interview the small talk is often focused around the interviewee's journey; and before a business meeting it could be to do with share prices. The subject of the small talk is not important; what is important is that it does take place. In many ways the more bland the topic, the safer it is likely to be, enabling both parties to operate on an equal basis. It is unlikely that one person will have a competitive advantage or significant expertise over the other person when talking about such subjects. It may be possible to find neutral topics that are of interest to both parties, for example the latest sports results or a recent news item.

A good next stage, having spent some time on small talk, is to try to find a subject that is of particular interest to the other person, and again invest some time in discussing this topic. A favourite, and one which is guaranteed to work in a Western culture, is the family and in particular the other person's children. Tread carefully with this subject in certain Eastern cultures though: the family tends to be a very private matter and taboo in business relationships. Sales executives are often taught systematically to gather non-work-related data on the other person and to make sure they demonstrate their personal knowledge of the client as soon as possible. This may seem rather mechanistic and phoney but there is some useful learning here about the power of being able to relate to the other person from his or her point of view. It is possible to be caught out, however, if you fake knowledge or understanding that you do not have; what do you do if the other person decides to discuss these subjects in depth? It could prove worthwhile, though, to know what the other person's favourite sport, pastime or team is; just a few exchanges on the right subject can accelerate the rapport-building process immensely.

SHOWING THE SIMILARITIES

Strong rapport builders are also very quick to pick up on areas of common interest or experience. They will identify such areas very early on simply by picking up on Johari arena-type information. They will then make a point of overtly declaring the common interest in order to identify with the other person. It is surprising the extent to which it is possible to find that you have something in common with the other even if he or she is quite different in personality and style.

As with first impressions where perception tends to be distorted, so our perception is distorted by a concept we will refer to as 'attracted to like'. This concept explains why, if we mingle freely amongst a mixed group of people in a large room, then after five or ten minutes we become attached to someone with a strong common bond. It may be that we come from the same town or that we have the same background, the same sporting interests, the same profession or the same educational background. In an influencing sense it is possible to use this perceptual distortion to ensure that the other person sees some common bond or identification with you as an influencer. Consider using the occasional expression like 'You are like me', 'I am like you in that sense' or 'That is where we are similar': this will not sound transparent and obvious if these comments are integrated with good identification of similarities.

USING SELF-DISCLOSURE

The next technique for building rapport plays on the fact that self-disclosure, as discussed in the Johari window model, can be a good way of building trust. If we are prepared to take the risk of disclosing some information that might normally be kept hidden behind the façade, then there can be some positive benefits. The chances are that the other person will feel that he or she can reciprocate and this is how trust is built gradually. Trust building is a process of reciprocal self-disclosure based on the premise that the other person will not abuse the privileged information he or she has. In the early stage of influencing a small amount of self-disclosure can help begin trust building. This could be as simple as sharing a concern or giving away some personal information. The emphasis is on a small amount of self-disclosure here because, if someone starts to disclose too much too soon, questions will be raised. The person on the receiving end of the self-disclosure could consider this as indicative of insecurity on the part of the discloser or that incorrect assumptions are being made about the nature of the relationship. Let's now bring these ideas together.

Storyboard: Making impact and building rapport

When James dressed, he carefully selected a suit that was in keeping with the client he was meeting later that day. He knew that the organization was highly traditional with conservative values, so he chose a grey pin-striped suit with white shirt and a simple dark blue tie.

Two hours later, he checked his appearance before he entered the office of his client. He smiled widely, and extended his hand in greeting. 'Good morning, Al. How are you?' (impact) 'Goodness, what a journey. It doesn't seem to get any easier – still it's nice to see you again. How's business?' (rapport)

James listened attentively whilst Al described the recent reorganization in the company. He tried not to interrupt, other than to seek clarification or to provide some empathetic response.

'You certainly have your hands full. I can't say I envy you. Never mind, think positively. You'll soon be on the Algarve with your family. Anyway, what can I do to help you?'(**rapport**)

After learning of the difficulty in introducing the new performance appraisal system, James said, 'I can see that the issue of communication would be a problem. However, when I worked for Ultracorp we had the same difficulty. We found that rather than viewing it as a communications problem, we treated it as a training issue.' (**self-disclosure: rapport**)

In many ways the above example demonstrates that issues like impact start in the competence of preparation, because if James had been inappropriately dressed he would not have created a positive first impression. In a similar way it can clearly be seen that the competence of impact involves human attentiveness skills like looking at the other person, greeting and smiling. Rapport is concerned with making the other person feel important. Techniques for doing this can vary from using the other person's name to asking what you can do to help.

Of course the other person may not want to engage in the process of rapport; instead he or she may wish to get straight to the point. In these circumstances, do not force the issue, but be prepared to respond to his or her specific needs. You may be able to build rapport at a later time. Rapport should never be rehearsed or it will appear stilted or false. It should focus on us picking up cues from either the other person or the current situation or circumstance.

Another method in building rapport is to establish some sort of banter with the other person; this could be fun discussion, or playful one-line comments. When you have sufficient confidence that your sense of humour will translate and that the other person will understand that you are taking a jovial approach, this can be a good technique. If in doubt, though, do not risk this approach. Unless the other person is on the same wavelength it may cause more problems than benefits. Humour does not generally travel well; while the use of understatement and irony tends to work well in a British culture, it may not translate to, say, a Germanic or Dutch culture where supposedly humorous comments are likely to be interpreted more literally.

We now consider further how relationships form using a different model.

A HIERARCHY OF **ATTRACTION**

An additional model for considering how relationships form, based on our research, suggests that relationships progress through several clearly defined stages, as follows:

1. awareness;
2. interest;
3. knowledge;
4. liking;
5. preference.

Awareness is about the other person becoming aware of our existence. This level is concerned primarily with making a positive impact and creating the appropriate first impression. **Interest** is the stage at which the other person identifies a value in the relationship; and **knowledge** is the level at which the other person is starting to gain a real understanding of our uniqueness as a human being. **Liking** occurs when the other person feels an affinity or closeness to us, probably as a result of recognizing similarities. At the highest level, **preference**, the other person identifies our unique ability to meet his or her needs, and influence is achieved as the other person trusts our integrity and readily accepts the suggestions we make.

We are frequently asked how long one should spend on the rapport stage of influencing; as a generalization, those managers with whom we have worked at developing the competences of influencing tend to spend far too little time creating rapport. Even if they do spend some time at the start, they will often move promptly into the 'real' business and assume that because some time has been spent developing rapport it will not be necessary to backtrack. Consequently the rest of the discussion focuses purely on the business in hand and not on developing trust.

A useful guideline in respect of how long to spend building rapport is to consider two key questions. First, how personal is the issue that we are going to discuss? Second, for how long am I likely to continue to work or have contact with this person after the discussion?

Where the answers to these questions are 'highly personal' and 'a long time', then the need to spend time creating rapport becomes paramount. For example, if I am about to discuss a personal habit of a colleague such as his or her need to use a body deodorant, then I will need to take much longer building rapport than I would if I was asking a service engineer to help me understand some new software.

Let's now consider the question of rapport in different cultural contexts. In what Trompenaars (1993) refers to as a 'specific' culture, such as that of the North American and Northern European countries, the main emphasis in a business relationship is placed on the business issues that have to be dealt with. The norm would be to spend a minimal amount of time on small talk because this could easily be seen as irrelevant. By contrast, in a 'diffuse' culture such that of the Latin, Arabic and South American countries, the emphasis is quite different. Here the relationship is considered to be with the whole person and it is not viewed as simply a contractual relationship. In this sort of diffuse culture rapport building could take months rather than minutes and, for someone used to the 'specific' environment, the danger would be showing impatience with the seemingly circuitous nature of early discussions. So one consideration when deciding how to build rapport is that of culture. Similarly, the concept of culture holds good in organizations. Some organizations you will recognize as 'diffuse' in nature while others may be more 'specific'.

Again in the context of trying to understand how relationships develop and the implications of this development on influencing, let's consider the stages through which relationships appear to pass on their way to becoming mature relationships.

MATURING RELATIONSHIPS

The model summarized in Figure 4.2 pulls the ideas of rapport and relationship development together.

We start by exploring initial encounters. When we meet an individual for the first time our behaviour could be described as **initiating**. This is about impact and rapport building. At this time, greetings will tend to be formal and special emphasis is placed on common courtesies. The interaction between both parties can be seen as controlled. There is no evidence of engaging in discussion of high-risk subjects. After some time the parties will move into what has been described as the **experimentation** stage. By this time they have become more relaxed and the interaction less formal. The range and scope of the conversation will extend beyond the professional and in this stage we begin to see the first signs of disclosure. By now humour may be present and spontaneity will be more the norm. Interestingly each can be seen as 'rewarding', helping and assisting the other.

Stabilizing is the next stage in this maturing relationship. By now there are high levels of self-disclosure. Others may see the individuals as a unit or team. There will be evidence of shared beliefs and values. Despite increased

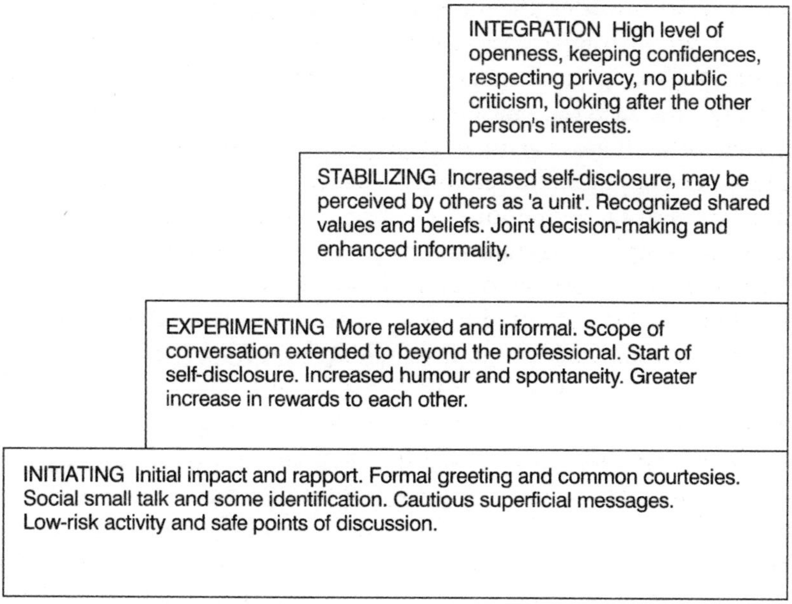

Figure 4.2 How relationships grow

informality, decision-making is perceived as a joint process. The final stage in this process is known as **integration**. By this stage there is a very high level of openness between both persons. Confidences will be kept and there will be a complete lack of public criticism of each other; indeed, each party will be seen to be supporting the needs of the other.

In this type of mature relationship the following behaviours can be observed:

■ Each rewards the other equally.
■ There is minimal blame.
■ Where disagreement occurs, both parties emphasize the importance of the relationship.
■ All differences are resolved using low-level confrontation, for example 'What can **we** do about this?'
■ High levels of personal disclosure.
■ Both are interested in each other as whole people, that is to say in all aspects of their lives.
■ Meaningful feedback is exchanged.

PAUSE FOR **THOUGHT**

1. *Think about someone you are trying to influence. Where is your relationship compared to stages in the above model?*
2. *What evidence have you got that supports your assessment of the stage at which the relationship is?*
3. *How is the stage you are at affecting your influencing approaches?*
4. *What can you do to move the relationship towards the next level?*

ATTENTION OR **AROUSAL**

So far in this chapter we have explored the competences of impact and rapport building. We now move on to consider the third competence of the chapter, the competence necessary for successful **preface**, noting that impact and rapport are closely linked to the skills of raising attention levels.

Attention or arousal can be defined as the acts and behaviours that are designed to draw attention to what we are about to say or do. It is about heightening the other person's interest. It is in many ways about drawing a line under the pleasantries stage and giving the signal that the real reason for the interaction is about to start. Attention can of course be gained by some physical act, for example, taking off a jacket or opening up a notebook; however, our experience suggests that these non-verbal behaviours are most powerful when used to support our language. Some of the most common ways of gaining attention, often observed as methods of drawing a metaphorical line, are as follows:

- Linking the preface with what has been discussed as part of the pleasantries stage, for example 'Well, you know you said you felt you didn't have enough budget. . .' (pause) 'well, I've got some ideas as to how we can reduce costs by 10 per cent.'
- Varying both intonation and volume of voice. Indeed, it has been shown that if we are talking normally, it gains interest if we change to talking more quietly.
- Using pre-empting statements, for example 'Do you want to know why this is important?' This approach is particularly powerful if the subject you are about to discuss is of personal interest to the other person, or if in some way it might be perceived as a treat. Likewise if you can appeal to the other person's value system this almost certainly will increase interest.
- Considering use of a prop if appropriate.
- Using a pause before and then after a statement has been made: you will be making silences work for you to raise levels of anticipation.

It is fairly common to see individuals failing to get the other person's interest because their voices are consistently quiet, or they speak in a monotone. Other common barriers include lack of energy (including non-verbal behaviours) and lack of excitement in the voice. A common failure is where a speaker gives too much information or bombards the other person with jargon. In either case the listener is likely to switch off.

The skill of maintaining attention levels is fundamentally about changing something in the environment. The need to do this to maintain interest is the product of our make-up. Take for example smells. When you enter a room you may well pick up a particular odour, say, a perfume or a smell of smoke. After a while, particularly if the smell is weak, it seems to disappear. This is because we accommodate to it so that it no longer registers in our consciousness. The same theory applies to maintaining attention. We need to change pace, tone, intonation or body language in order to maintain arousal and prevent accommodation. Another effective way of doing this, in addition to the ideas described above, is summarizing. This technique increases attention as people look to pick up the key points covered in your conversation. OK, in summary then!

So far we have explored the first two stages of the Model of Successful Influencing and within that we have considered the competences of preparation (information gathering and mental readiness), impact, rapport building and arousal and maintaining of attention. We will presently move on to the **position** and **problems** stage of the model and in particular focus on the competence of understanding. Before doing this, you are invited to consider the following questions, which will help you develop your skills of arousal and maintaining interest.

PAUSE FOR **THOUGHT**

1. *How do you maintain people's interest when you are in conversations?*
2. *What do you see other people doing in order to heighten audience interest and attention?*
3. *What ideas are you going to use to maintain interest when you are engaged in influencing conversations?*

five

POSITION AND
PROBLEMS

By the end of this chapter the reader will:

- recognize the importance of engaging in a dynamic, evolving two-way process at the stage of position and problems;
- know how to massage problems and be able to use a framework for isolating and prioritizing problems;
- be able to state the common barriers to listening, and describe the hierarchy of the skills of active listening;
- know the different types of questions, and be able to describe the technique of three-level questioning.

INTRODUCTION

We have reviewed the skills of preparation, pleasantries and preface. We now consider the 'hand in glove' skills of questioning and listening that major in the position and problems stage of the influencing process. In this chapter, we explore listening and questioning by revisiting the issue of influencing styles and describing questioning types. We then explore listening skills introducing NLP (more information later), provide models for problem identification and introduce the idea of joint vision statements.

PUSH V PULL **STYLES**

Try this: hold up the palm of your hand and ask your friend to do the same; do not tell him or her anything, but slowly start pressing towards the other person. What happens? Nine times out of ten, the other person will resist or push back at you. As you intensify the strength of your push he or she is likely to match you. What you are seeing is really the equivalent of what frequently happens when we are attempting to influence others. We push our view, they push theirs and the more strongly they push theirs, the more strongly we push ours.

If the other person has a point of view to which we are diametrically opposed, then a natural reaction is to present vehemently our counter-argument. The problem with this push approach, though, is that it is quite possible to misunderstand the other person's view or to miss out on a different perspective which could be enlightening. The key competences, which we need to develop in order to avoid this pitfall, are those of listening and questioning.

Listening in an influencing context is to do with more than just hearing; it is about understanding the words and interpreting the messages being conveyed. Furthermore, it is not sufficient to remain content in the knowledge that we have listened effectively; in influencing, we must demonstrate to the other person that we have understood the message as it was intended. This should not of course be confused with agreement.

You might argue that a negotiating tactic would be to summarize incorrectly what the other person has said, adding your own interpretation, but remember, we are addressing here the position and problems stage of the model. The critical competence at this stage is **understanding**.

Listening and questioning can both be approached at various levels and we will look at how, through deeper-level listening and questioning skills, it is possible to understand not just the message but the feelings, emotions, motives and underlying values of the person you are attempting to influence. In order to influence effectively it is vital to understand the other person and have a clear picture of his or her perspective. It is only when we are armed with this understanding that it becomes possible to use what is important to that person as a way of influencing rather than use an influencing strategy based on what is important to us. The latter strategy is in effect coercion.

Finally in this chapter we will look at how to summarize our understanding of problems and position, and at establishing a joint vision which allows the outcome sought by both parties to be achieved. This can be expressed in terms of a joint output statement.

QUESTIONS WHICH PRODUCE **RESULTS**

One of the major misconceptions about questioning skills is that there are hard and fast rules about which sorts of questions to use. In the context of influencing, this is simply not the case. The successful influencer needs to be aware of a whole range of kinds of question and should be able to use different types according to, first, his or her objective and, second, the nature and style of the other person. So while it may be necessary to ask open-ended questions in order to understand fully someone else's point of view, asking such questions of a person who needs help in structuring his or her conversation because of a tendency to digress, will simply fuel the problem.

Here we will look at the use of questions as a method of gaining understanding of the other's perspective. Later in the book we will consider the issue of questions that address the subject from a rather different point of view, that is, the use of certain types of question in order to persuade or lead the other party to accept your ideas or proposals.

There are a number of categories of question that can be used at the **diagnosis** stage of an influencing situation. Each is considered below.

INFORMATIONAL QUESTIONS

The informational question aims to draw the person out by phrasing the question in such a way that he or she is unable to respond with brief answers and is obliged to provide information regarding his or her own perspective. Such questions tend to be prefaced with words such as 'How. . .', 'Why. . .' or 'Tell me. . .'.

The intention of the questioner is not to make judgements or to present his or her own view at this stage, but simply to understand where the other person is coming from. Listening skills are also critical. In handling the response, it is essential to assist the speaker with supportive, but neutral, words and gestures such as selective head nods, saying 'uh huh' or 'mm mm', or comments which demonstrate listening like 'I see' and 'I understand'.

Some examples of how informational questions might be phrased are:

■ 'Tell me about it.'
■ 'How do you feel about this?'
■ 'What are your views on. . .?'
■ 'What do you mean by. . .?'
■ 'Is there anything else?'

This sort of question makes it rather difficult to evade the issue and withhold information unless the person is being deliberately awkward. Such questions are particularly relevant when it is proving difficult to gain information, either because others are naturally introverted and quiet or because tactically they are 'playing their cards close to their chest'.

Some caution needs to be taken with those who have a natural tendency to talk. They may be normally extroverted or they may be trying to baffle you with lots of information; in this case asking informational questions which are not sufficiently focused can serve to exacerbate the situation.

PROBING QUESTIONS

Probing questions seek to explore a particular subject in some depth. Probes might start in the following ways:

- 'Can you give me some examples?'
- 'In what way. . .?'
- 'Specifically, what was your role?'
- 'What did you enjoy or not enjoy about. . .?'
- 'What evidence do you have for that?'
- 'Tell me more.'
- 'How would you support this comment?'

The aim with a probing type of question is to seek more information on a subject that has been discussed superficially. It is about trying to ascertain the depth of understanding. Certain comments or non-verbal behaviours may trigger a need to probe. It could be that the person seems a little evasive or cautious, or you may be picking up signals that suggest he or she is withholding important information or even being 'economical with the truth'. In these circumstances it is necessary to probe, and to demonstrate that you are not going to accept anything other than the whole story.

You may find that the individual presents you with a 'neon sign' statement. As mentioned earlier, these are statements that invite you to ask another question. Frequently they are used because the person does not want to raise an issue explicitly, but would prefer you to ask the question. Examples are: 'I would have been on time but things have been difficult recently'; and 'That is a valid point but there are other issues at play here.' In the first example, the person might have been unwell and is using this as an excuse for explaining away work that is late; however, he or she does not want to be seen as making excuses. In the second example, the person is stating that there were other factors, and is indicating that you should ask about them.

These sorts of statement beg for a probing response. However, a word of caution: sometimes people will present you with neon signs in order to be able to respond in a manipulative manner. When we become aware that we are seeing a neon sign, we do not have to respond to it necessarily. We might just note it and come back to the issue later.

A useful technique to use if you are getting short answers when attempting to probe is to phrase questions in relative terms in order to seek comparisons. For example, a question such as 'Which of the reports are you more comfortable with and which are you less comfortable with?' followed by a 'Why?' will draw out more information than 'Which is your favourite report?' to which a respondent could more easily say, 'I don't have a preference.'

BEHAVIOURAL QUESTIONS

A behavioural question seeks information about how an individual behaves in a specific situation. Behavioural questions need to be focused on real situations. They provide evidence of actual behaviour drawn from experience rather than in hypothetical situations. The difficulty with a hypothetical or 'What would you do if. . .?' type of question is that it often elicits a response based on how the respondents would like to see themselves behaving rather than on how they would really behave: the two are not always the same.

Seeking information about previous behaviours is the best predictor of how a person is likely to behave in the future. This approach can provide valuable information about the nature of the person you are influencing. For example, if you are able to predict how he or she might respond in a certain situation based on past behaviours, then this information can be used to shape your influencing strategy.

Examples of behavioural questions are:

- 'Tell me about a situation where you had to cope without resources and under a time pressure. What happened? How did you cope? What did you do?'
- 'Tell me about how you responded when your staff were upset about the reorganization. What did you do? What did you say? How did you handle it? What was the most difficult aspect of this incident?'
- 'How did you persuade your boss to increase your budget? What did you do? What was your approach? What objections were there? How did you handle them?'

PINPOINT QUESTIONS

Pinpoint questions seek specific information and fall into two categories. First, there is the direct question for those occasions when you want to clarify specific information. In this case the response is likely to be short and factual. An example of a pinpoint clarification question is 'So are you saying the price is $3,000 including service or excluding service?' This leaves little room for manoeuvre on the part of the respondent and enables the questioner to fill in pieces of the jigsaw.

Second, there are questions that seek to deal with the deliberately vague statements often made by others in an effort to exert influence and add weight to their arguments. Pinpoint questions in this situation cause the speaker to clarify and indeed justify his or her comments. They aim to pinpoint missing or vague areas and may even cause the speaker to come forward with information that could otherwise have been withheld. The only problem with pinpoint questions is that they can often sound too direct and abrupt, and the danger is that without some 'dressing up' to soften them, any rapport which has previously been established can be destroyed quickly. Some examples of the phrases to look out for and to tackle with pinpoint questions are shown below. Examples of appropriate pinpoint questions are given and then examples of how the questions might be dressed up in order to maintain rapport. Also important to the rapport issue is the way in which the question is asked. The intonation, facial expressions and body language of the questioner determine this. A supportive and interested style is more appropriate than an abrupt style, which may be interpreted as hostile.

Below are examples that bring these ideas to life. We give typical instances of the kinds of things people say where a pinpoint question is required – vague descriptions, sweeping generalizations, exaggerations and definitive statements – and then describe pinpoint questions and how you might dress those questions up.

Vague descriptions

'They keep pushing me around.'

Pinpoint questions:	Who are they?
	What do you mean pushing around?
	Could you give some examples?
	How often does it happen?
Dressed up:	I understand it must feel pretty uncomfortable. . . Who are the main people causing the problem? What do they do? How often does this sort of thing happen?

Sweeping generalizations

'Everybody knows she is always complaining – she will find anything to complain about.'

Pinpoint questions:	Everybody. . . have you interviewed everybody on this personally? What do you mean always? When did she last complain? What was the reason?
Dressed up:	That sounds tiresome. I know it would irritate me if someone kept complaining. What does she complain about? Have you got any examples?

Exaggeration

'He is the world's worst dresser.'

Pinpoint questions:	World's worst? Surely not?
Dressed up:	His dress sense may need some attention. What specifically do you feel the problem is? Is it to do with style or colour co-ordination for example?

Definitive statements

'We could never get approval.'

Pinpoint questions:	Who said? Have you tried? Never ever?
Dressed up:	Yes, it must be tricky in this climate. I wonder if it might at some stage get easier?

USING THREE-LEVEL **QUESTIONING**

Figure 5.1 shows how a line of questioning might be developed in the attempt to identify other people's values. It is a process of digging ever deeper, continuing to ask why they do what they do.

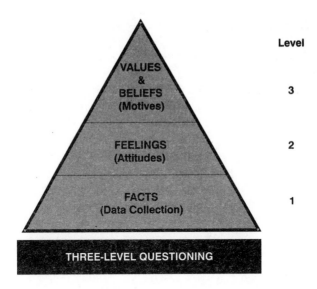

Figure 5.1 Three-level questioning

As discussed previously, being able to identify the core values driving the person you are attempting to influence has major advantages in that it is then possible to use this knowledge in formulating an appropriate influencing strategy. Techniques which approach influencing by appealing to the other person's value system are likely to be much more successful than attempting to impose one's own values.

The three-level questioning model suggests, as its name indicates, that there are broadly three levels at which it is possible to question. Level 1 describes data, level 2 feelings and attitudes, and level 3 values and beliefs. An example, if one is attempting to identify core values in order to influence another person in a conversation, could be:

Storyboard: Levels of questioning

PIERRE: So tell me a little more about what you do. (**Level 1**)
MARIANNE: Oh, I work as a sales executive. We sell pharmaceutical products, mainly to hospitals and clinics.
PIERRE: Interesting. What sort of products are you involved with? (**Level 1**)
MARIANNE: Well, it's mainly vaccines and some of the new drugs for inoculation of children.

> PIERRE: So what does this mean for you? (**Level 2**)
> MARIANNE: Actually it means a lot of time away from home. Lots of travel – visiting all sorts of different organizations – hospitals, clinics, day centres. To be honest, despite all the hassle, I really enjoy it.
> PIERRE: What is it you particularly enjoy? (**Level 2**)
> MARIANNE: What gives me the most satisfaction is the fact that I personally decide where I go and who to meet. I have a great deal of scope to decide the sales strategy. If I want to do something, I just do it. It really is so different from my last company where everything I did had to be approved by a director. I couldn't even get approval for a car phone, and I was a sales executive, on the road 80 per cent of the time.
> PIERRE: So why is it so important for you to be able to decide on where you go and who you meet? (**Level 3**)
> MARIANNE: That's a tricky question – I guess it's to do with independence. I've always had this need to do my own thing. I've always wanted to be my own boss. I just can't stand feeling constrained. I truly believe that everyone has potential if they're allowed to get on with it, instead of people interfering.

What Pierre has identified through this process of three-level questioning is that Marianne has a core value of independence. In attempting to influence her, it would be important to emphasize the fact that she would have scope and personal discretion; the danger to guard against would be imposing too much control on her. This could have been quite different; for instance, if Marianne had revealed a strong need for security and safety, then there being close supervision on which to fall back would have been an important point to make.

ACTIVE **LISTENING**

As the first learnt and most used of communication skills, it is surprising that listening is the least taught. 'Listening' is one of the most misused terms. Have you ever had the experience of someone saying 'Carry on, I'm listening' and you hesitate to continue because you are not convinced that they actually are listening? Conversely have you ever been in conversation with someone else and found your mind wandering on to another subject or tuning in to someone else's conversation? Have you had a discussion with someone close to you where they have said 'But you just don't understand'? If so, then you have experienced personally some of the difficulties associated with listening.

Listening breaks down for several reasons. It may be that the person trying to get you to listen is sending more information than you can digest at one time. In this situation it is not helpful to blame the speaker as you have a joint responsibility to ensure that the process of communication is effective. One approach is to help the speaker by giving structure to the discussion with interventions that address the process of the discussion, for instance: 'I am having some difficulty following you here – could we first of all cover subject x and then move on to y?' Or it may be appropriate to ask the speaker if he or she minds if you take a few notes, which incidentally will buy you more time to think as you are writing.

Emotions are entering the world of management; take for example Goleman's widely acclaimed books on emotional intelligence. Emotions, however, can easily get in the way of effective listening and it may be better to admit to the other person that you are feeling angry, upset or even too overjoyed to be able to listen properly. This is about recognizing your own emotional state and the effect it is having on you and on your ability to listen. Often, in order to listen effectively, it helps to take some time out and come back to the subject when the emotion has subsided. Sometimes just one word used by the other person can have major emotional impact, often for personal reasons. This may be related to powerful previous experiences, good or bad, which come flooding back and obstruct the listening process. Try to recognize your emotional state and work with it. Emotions are powerful things; they drive our actions and perceptions, and motivate us. Recognizing our own changing emotional state in a dialogue and being able to recognize that of the other party are key facets of emotional intelligence and understanding when influencing.

Another reason for failure to listen could be related to who is speaking; if we do not like that person or have a certain opinion of his or her worth or value, then we are likely to give the same value to what he or she says. Or it could be that we categorize the other person in terms of a stereotype. We are all susceptible to the dangers of stereotyping, that is the tendency to label other people or make generalized assumptions. 'We fit people into the stereotypical image for that category of person. Stereotypes are based around a number of issues such as gender, race, religion, age, and profession or occupation. It is, however, possible to make serious misjudgements about people because of the tendency to stereotype' (Hale, 1993).

We may have a stereotyped view of academics that they all lack common sense and tend to be preoccupied with theory. If we are perhaps given a piece of practical and relevant advice by an academic, we might dismiss it before listening to it. The key here is to recognize which stereotypes you hold and how they can get in the way of understanding the individual.

It is also important to note that other people hold stereotyped views of you, and it is therefore useful to consider how these may get in the way of our influencing.

PAUSE FOR **THOUGHT**

1. *What type of questions do you usually use?*
2. *How effective are they at giving you a real understanding of the other person and his or her values?*
3. *What can you do to improve your listening skills? Make a commitment to try out our ideas.*
4. *On what are the stereotypes that others might have of you based?*
5. *What parts of these stereotypes do you perceive as positive and what parts negative?*
6. *What if anything can you do to optimize the positive aspects of the stereotype whilst minimizing the negative aspects?*

Another common cause of failure to listen is what psychologists refer to as 'cognitive dissonance', which is described as 'the feeling of discomfort that a person has when he or she holds conflicting attitudes towards the same stimulus' (Wittig and Belkin, 1990). It explains how we process opposing internal viewpoints. For instance, if someone holds the two viewpoints, 'Drinking and driving wrecks lives' and 'I am a more confident and competent driver after a few drinks', then the feeling of discomfort becomes so intense that one of the beliefs will be eliminated. When listening, we often receive conflicting messages from the other person and therefore fail to receive the real message. Take for example this situation: you are used to someone always giving you good news, and he or she then tries to give you bad news. When this happens you may fail to hear the real message accurately because you are tuned in to that person giving good news.

Another major factor affecting one's ability to listen is driven by the characteristics of memory and recall. We introduced this issue in Chapter 1 when we explored the normal level of attention and recall of information over a period of time. We showed that during the period of an input the listener tends to be more attentive at the start and end with some high peaks of attention and recall throughout. This is known as the von Restorff effect.

We will now look more closely at how we listen. Figure 5.2 shows the common response of someone listening to a speaker in a one-to-one discussion. This shows that when a speaker is talking, the listener typically spends the first part of the input listening, the second part formulating and the final part trying to gain entry to the discussion. This has implications for how effective the listening is. If the speaker is presenting an argument or point of view with which the listener disagrees then the listening time may be reduced further. The implication for the speaker is that the key message needs to be delivered succinctly and early on.

We now explore the concept of levels of listening in order to help you develop your listening abilities. As with questioning levels, our research suggests that we can operate at three levels of listening: basic, intermediate and advanced. Figure 5.3 illustrates this diagrammatically.

Basic

At a basic level listening is about 'shutting up' or stopping talking. This is an obvious but often neglected first step and should be accompanied by concentration on what the speaker is saying. In terms of body language the behaviours which should support concentration are selective head nods and supportive noises such as 'uh huh' and 'mm mm'; most people tend to do this without even thinking about it but have you ever had the experience of talking where the listener provides no supportive noises? It can be quite

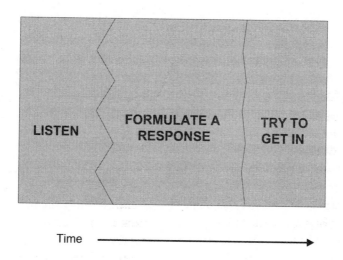

LISTEN   FORMULATE A RESPONSE   TRY TO GET IN

Time

Figure 5.2 One-to-one listening

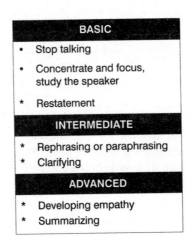

* indicates an active listening response

Figure 5.3 Levels of listening

disconcerting, and if it happens when you are communicating by telephone you might wonder whether the person is still on the other end of the line. You don't have the benefit of being able to look at the other person for feedback.

At a basic level it can be helpful simply to restate what the speaker says, though clearly some caution needs to be exercised because simply repeating the last few words like an echo can be irritating if overworked. Repeating key words and then pausing, though, can prove to be a very good way of assisting speakers and encouraging them to give more information. This is a technique often used to good effect by interviewers. Watch how interviewers in the media use these techniques.

Intermediate

At an intermediate level the techniques of listening involve paraphrasing what the other person is saying. Paraphrasing means reflecting what the other person has said using your own words, without changing the meaning. By doing this it is possible to check that you have received the message correctly, which can be reassuring for both speaker and listener. Seeking clarification on a specific point is another aspect of listening and a way of demonstrating that you are engaged and understanding.

Advanced

At an advanced level listening is about developing empathy with the speaker. Empathy can be defined as 'the quality of feeling as another feels, to experience another's reality from that other person's point of view' (Wittig and Belkin, 1990). In a normal discussion the two parties tend to focus on the content of the discussion, and there may be an undercurrent of emotions and feelings experienced by both parties. Often these emotions are never discussed, because an assumption is made that one should keep focused on the discussion in hand. Showing empathy means seeking to identify how the other person feels about what he or she is describing and then demonstrating that you understand the feeling. If it is possible to demonstrate genuinely that you have an understanding of the feeling he or she is experiencing, by mentioning your own similar experience, then this will enhance the relationship. It shows empathy through the techniques of identification and self-disclosure. Both support the development of trust and the growth of the relationship.

A three-step approach to showing empathy is:

1. Recognize the emotion (eg is the other person angry, excited, upset, frustrated, sad, etc?).
2. Check that you have interpreted the emotion correctly (eg 'You seem pleased about this' or 'This has clearly upset you').
3. Show understanding and empathy (eg 'I can understand how you might feel. I had a similar experience and I was also upset').

As previously discussed, sometimes the other person will signal in a subtle way that he or she is seeking to disclose some information, particularly if the subject is tricky or personal in nature. Often the signal is hidden in some seemingly innocuous statement that it is hoped you will pick up on so that he or she can then disclose more information; we previously referred to these statements as 'neon signs'. In themselves they mean nothing, but they may prompt you to ask exactly what is meant so that more information can be disclosed; they tend to be used when someone has something important to say but does not quite know how to get into discussion of the subject.

PAUSE FOR THOUGHT: **EMPATHY**

Demonstrating empathy, develop a response to the statements below. Remember you will need to identify the feeling, show that you recognize it and find some way of identifying with it.

At this stage we are just focusing on a response which shows empathy, not attempting to solve the problem or even make recommendations. This is something that might follow after having demonstrated understanding and empathy.

Example:
   'I keep getting interrupted; I'm simply not getting enough done and I'm slipping behind schedule.'

Empathy response:
   'I can imagine you must feel quite frustrated; I know when I've had to work on important projects and was disturbed I ended up feeling very stressed.'

Statements
1. *'I just cannot handle any more of this – I'm working in lunch hours and after hours. I have a life outside of work too, you know.'*
2. *'We've got this really important meeting tomorrow, and I know the senior management are going to be there. I really haven't got all my information together. I know I'm not as well prepared as I should be, but I've just been so busy lately.'*
3. *'Everybody's talking about changes around here. I even heard that the chief executive's leaving. Nobody knows what to believe any more. You just don't know what's likely to happen – the next target could be our department.'*
4. *'They broke into my car and not only did they take the radio but they even stole my work case. I mean, what use is that to them? I just cannot believe what society is coming to.'*
5. *'I've been working for six months now without a break. And the amount of work has been building up gradually over that time. What's more, family life hasn't been too easy, what with the new baby and the house move.'*
6. *'Instead of just leaving me to do it my way, everyone seems to have some smart suggestion about how things could be done better. Why don't other people keep their noses out of my business and let me try my best? OK, if I get it wrong then that's my problem and I'm prepared to accept the consequences.'*
7. *'It's really strange, before I retired I was so busy and now life just seems kind of empty. The other thing is, people used to recognize me and give me a good level of respect. Now I'm just the same as the man on the street.'*
8. *'Only one week to go and then I've a month touring around the world. I just can't wait – I'm counting the hours. I don't know how I'm going to contain myself over the next few days. And the other thing is, it means it's extremely difficult to concentrate on work.'*

Clearly not all your message is transmitted by the words you use. It is vital that you consider body language, in particular non-verbal cues given and received. When talking to others, we normally check and track their behaviour and tend to adjust our behaviour accordingly. In a similar way the listener engages in what is described by psychologists as 'backchannel behaviour'. This involves the observer reviewing, often subconsciously, the non-verbal cues of the speaker to see if the words match the body language. Interestingly research has shown that where there might be discrepancies between what is being said and the accompanying behaviour, the non-verbal aspects will be accorded higher value. Such discrepancies between body language and verbal message often lead to us mistrusting the speaker or indeed lead to us believing that the speaker is being untruthful. This brings us to the subject of understanding at a higher level.

UNDERSTANDING AT A HIGHER **LEVEL**

An advanced form of listening and understanding has been developed as part of the concept of neuro-linguistic programming (NLP). Richard Bandler, a mathematician, psychotherapist and computer specialist, and John Grinder, a linguist, developed this in the early 1970s. They studied the work of leading psychotherapists who were consistent in their ability to facilitate powerful and lasting change and personal improvements in others. NLP focuses on close study of the behaviours that support the positive development of relationships between people. Whilst some aspects of NLP can seem rather tangential to the business environment, there are some interesting and relevant concepts concerning how to understand the thought processes of others.

It has been shown that through understanding how the person we are attempting to influence thinks, we can improve rapport and build the relationship. This approach may be seen as an advanced form of listening as it proposes that we can detect and then use some of the very subtly disclosed clues which the speaker will reveal about his or her thought processes.

The 'neuro' part of neuro-linguistic programming refers to the neurological processes of the five senses, that is, seeing, hearing, feeling, tasting and smelling. It is believed that humans use the senses to help with their internal thought processes just as much as to experience external factors. The term 'linguistic' refers to the way that people use language to organize internal thought processes; and 'programming' indicates that thoughts and behaviour can be managed actively.

In NLP terms, the use of certain senses tends to dominate our thinking and this is often revealed in terms of the language we use. Our thinking preferences may be biased towards any of the following senses, though normally the dominant tendency will be towards one of the first three:

- sight (visual);
- sound (auditory);
- touch (kinaesthetic);
- smell (olfactory);
- taste (gustatory).

People tend to use words in speech that suggest their preference in terms of thinking. So comments and expressions such as:

- 'I see what you mean';
- 'I can picture the person';
- 'We should look at this. . .';
- 'Its a black picture';
- 'You must keep things in perspective';
- 'She's a colourful character';

would reveal a preference towards visual thought processes. Comments and phrases such as:

- 'The message is received loud and clear';
- 'This behaviour is unheard of';
- 'It just sounds right';
- 'It's music to my ear';
- 'His clothes are so loud';

would suggest an auditory bias. Comments and phrases such as:

- 'Let's touch base on this';
- 'It doesn't feel right';
- 'He's a smooth character';
- 'Don't push me';
- 'We need to pull him into line';

would suggest a predominantly kinaesthetic thinking preference.

Clearly we use all of our senses to some degree in our thinking, but it is likely that if our language were monitored over a period of time, then a predominant thinking preference would emerge. Furthermore, there are other ways of identifying thinking preferences, by interpreting non-verbal signals: so a visual thinker will tend to look up when speaking, an auditory person will tend to 'sing' more when talking and a kinaesthetic thinker will tend to speak in a slower, deeper tone, keeping the head down. Again these non-verbal signals are general guidelines rather than absolutes.

The benefit of this knowledge is that if we can identify the other person's thinking preferences then it is possible to strengthen the sense of rapport by using similar sensory styles in our own speech; this is often referred to as mirroring. So the following examples are ways of saying the same thing but making adjustments to suit the thinking preference of the other person.

- Visual: 'Can you picture the situation if you take this option? It will really bring some colour to the department.'
- Auditory: 'I can hear the reaction now – they'll be singing out with joy.'
- Kinaesthetic: 'It's bound to trigger some action – it's the sort of kick that they all need.'

It may take some time to be able to pick up (note the kinaesthetic phrase) the signals and to formulate relevant responses, but with practice this will become more natural, and in the meantime you can have some fun identifying the thought patterns of others. This is an advanced approach to listening, one which might be described as a 'meta-listening' strategy that seeks to listen to information over and above the obvious subject matter and to tune into (an auditory phrase) the other person's thought processes.

We have now provided you with information, models and ideas on questioning and listening skills. What do you do with the information you gather through these skills? We are entering the territory of problem solving. Below are some problem-solving tools that you can use in collaboration with another party in order to develop a way forward or a joint vision.

PROBLEM-DEFINING **TOOLS**

Massaging the problem

The first of these process tools is massaging the problem. It will help you generate an understanding of the issues by providing a framework that captures the issues. Massaging problems uses the matrix given in Table 5.1.

PAUSE FOR **THOUGHT**

1. *Think about a situation you want to influence.*
2. *Fill in the gaps with the known, and then develop questions that begin to explore the unknown.*
3. *When you have gathered your information, start to identify the alternatives that exist, using your questions, either jointly with the person you are trying to influence or on your own.*

Table 5.1 Massaging problems

	Critical examination of the issues			
	Current facts	Reasons	Possible alternatives	Review purpose
WHAT	What is done now?	Why is it done	What *else* could be done?	What *should* be done?
HOW	How is it done?	Why in that way?	How *else* could it be done?	How *should* it be done?
WHEN	When is it done?	Why at that time?	When *else* could it be done?	When *should* it be done?
WHERE	Where is it done?	Why in that place?	Where *else* could it be done?	Where *should* it be done?
WHO	Who does it?	Why that person?	Who *else* could do it?	Who *should* do it?

Why, why, why?

In a similar way, it is possible to use a 'why why' diagram as a method of defining the cause of a problem, rather that just dealing with the effect. A worked example of this is shown in Figure 5.4 where the issue of poor product sales is probed in order to define the problem.

Again, using this approach with a real influencing situation will help you to develop an understanding of the issues and identify what you really need to focus on. If you use these techniques on your own before or after a meeting with the person you are trying to influence then you will develop clarity on what needs to be done. If you use these tools collaboratively with the person you are trying to influence, then the next step is the development of a joint vision.

BUILDING A JOINT **VISION**

Finally in this chapter we will look at how to analyse the information gained through questioning and listening. We will look at how this understanding of the position and the problem can be developed into a jointly agreed outcome statement.

Having used the diagnostic skills of listening and questioning effectively, and having clarified the issues using one of the problem-defining tools, you now need to develop a way forward. This is done by considering how the other person's understanding of the situation matches your own.

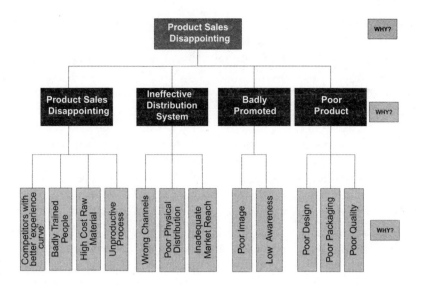

Figure 5.4 The 'why why' method

When this has been 'put on the table', you can then develop a joint vision statement.

Why overtly agree the desired outcome? Too often the different parties will approach an influencing situation with different outcomes in mind. This may not even become apparent until it is too late. We therefore hold the view that early joint exploration of desired outcomes leads to more effective resolutions.

We suggest that parties in the influencing situation should seek to develop outcome statements, which describe what a successful outcome looks like. The intention is to build jointly a picture of success that both parties can buy into. In an informal situation, which is limited by time, it may be possible only to agree this verbally through a brief discussion.

Examples of outcome statements are: 'We are going to agree the rates for this contract in a way which pleases both parties so that we can continue to build our successful business relationship'; or 'We will find a way to overcome the grievance you have raised so that you remain suitably motivated to continue to enrich the work of the department.'

The outcome statement should be phrased in a positive way that highlights the desired result rather than dwelling unduly on the negative aspects of the existing situation. The difference is subtle but important; it should state what is wanted rather than what is to be avoided or overcome. This helps both parties move towards a successful outcome. The process of jointly building the outcome statement can have an integrating effect in itself. By involving the other person in agreeing its wording, he or she is more likely to feel committed to working towards it.

We have now considered the key skills associated with the position and problem stage of the model. Understanding is about ensuring that the problem or issue is discussed from the other person's perspective before making any potentially dangerous assumptions. This can mean a measure of self-control, particularly if the other person seems to have a very different perspective from your own. Objective questioning and strong listening skills will be called for in all influencing situations. We have looked at a number of techniques here. As expressed at the start of this book, listening and questioning skills remain essential throughout the influencing process but they major in this area of understanding.

You are now at the stage where you are able to describe the current position, drawing on your clear and sound understanding of the other person's point of view and his or her aims. You will have begun to clarify and integrate the different views into a mutually acceptable outcome statement. So what next? Presently we will explore possibilities and preferences but before we do we highlight the findings of recent studies on effective communication.

RESEARCH **FINDINGS**

Recent studies (Whetton and Cameron, 1996) have shown that effective communication appears to have the following characteristics:

- focusing on problems rather than personalities;
- absence of being judgmental;
- active listening;
- strong consistency between verbal and non-verbal behaviour;
- positive recognition and regard for the other person's contribution.

These are all ideas we support strongly and ones that have a particular relevance when trying to develop understanding. In this chapter, we have suggested that you focus on the issue, and have highlighted the importance of active listening, consistency in your message and a collaborative approach. These ideas remain important throughout the influencing process. Holding these ideas in mind, let's now explore the next stage of the Model of Successful Influencing, possibilities and preferences.

POSSIBILITIES, PREFERENCES AND
POSITIVE ACTION

In this chapter we:

- explore the issues of manipulation v influence;
- discuss the distinction between logical and emotional approaches to persuasion;
- continue to explore issues of impressions management;
- examine the competences of building personal credibility as well as the techniques of verbal persuasion;
- consider the process of positive action;
- recognize the importance of providing feedback to others.

In this chapter, we will look at the detailed techniques used by some of the most influential people we have met in our research. These techniques are often subtly deployed but let there be no doubt that they are used consistently by those with the power of personal influence.

It could be argued that the use of such techniques in order to persuade others smacks of manipulation. To explore this, it would help to agree a working definition of the term 'manipulation' in order to define clearly the approach we are advocating in the influencing context. We would define manipulation as: **'The use of covert techniques, where the aim is to confuse or deceive another person or persons with malicious intent, in order to gain an advantage for self or others.'**

The important point in the interpretation of this definition is that manipulation may describe an approach which aims to result in an 'I win, you lose' outcome. Often people who are manipulative will use other people and create circumstances that allow them to achieve their goals. That their goals are seldom declared means that the person being subjected to such manipulation is often an innocent victim and there is usually some dishonest intent. Let's look at a real example.

Storyboard: The manipulative manager

Steven was determined to get his boss to accept the need for a trip to the parent company in California, USA. However he realized that this needed to be within the next few months as he knew next year's budget was going to be tight.

He considered he deserved the trip. After all most of his colleagues had managed to visit the plant, and by all accounts had had a great time in the process. It was generally accepted that such a trip was part of the senior management reward package. Steven knew that getting this finance was not going to be easy, primarily because of all the recent overhead reductions.

On thinking this over Steven realized that his only real chance of getting finance for the trip would be to try to use existing money, rather than attempting to get hold of a new budget. His best hope seemed to be to cancel a forthcoming planned training programme and to reallocate its budget to allow him his visit.

Sue was his subordinate manager, and it was she who had originally wanted the course. She was extremely keen to provide training for all her department particularly in the area of improving team work, and she had been instrumental in designing the training programme. She had used an agency to identify a suitable venue, which she had publicly stated she felt to be most critical as it was crucial to create the correct environment in issues of team building.

Steven knew he would find it difficult arbitrarily to cancel the training, particularly as his boss seemed to be increasingly keen on training. Consequently he needed to get the line manager to cancel the event, while at the same time absolving himself of any responsibility.

He arranged to meet with Sue, and before the actual meeting he let it be implied, via one of her colleagues (**third party influencing**), that he wanted to discuss a couple of matters of serious (**power word**) concern about the forthcoming training event (**attitude structuring**).

Although Steven had no strong feelings either way as to the value or otherwise of such training, he started the meeting by vociferously supporting the concept of team building (**enhanced personal**

---

credibility). He also acknowledged Sue's previous comments about the importance of the venue (**supportive**) as the critical factor enabling a successful outcome (**anxiety provocation**).

He then said: 'I heard from my friend Bill (**valued third party reference**) over at INCO that they used the same hotel. However, they were very, very (**repetition**) unhappy at the level of service. Apparently they found that there was a big difference between the rhetoric and the reality.' (**alliteration**)

He went on to say: 'I know you wouldn't want this to be a failure (**assumption**), not least because you're doing so well at the moment.' (**coercive threat**)

Sue was clearly worried: 'What are the alternatives?' Steven moves closer and his voice becomes almost conspiratorial. He says: 'We have several options. Let's not rush anything.' (**collaborative**)

Sue agrees in principle but seems hesitant. Steven keeps repeating the message: 'Let's not rush anything.' (**repetition**)

While she is thinking out these issues, Steven starts to throw out a list of other questions (**discrepancy**): 'Is the agenda finalized? What arrangements have been made for the briefing? How are we going to measure success? Who else have you got to support the programme? How are we justifying the costs?'

These additional issues seem to be distracting Sue from the apparent original difficulties of the hotel.

Clearly Steven's tactic is not to give her time to think while at the same time raising her anxiety level (**anxiety acceleration**), and having done this he ultimately offers her a lifeline (**psychological relief**) by suggesting the training should be postponed until these issues can be successfully resolved.

Steven further adds: 'If we postpone the programme by, say, six months, then maybe we can pull in some of the other teams.'

After a few minutes more of these sorts of manipulative persuasive techniques, Sue agrees that postponing the programme until some of the issues have been resolved is the best solution.

Even now Steven can feel that Californian sun!

What is apparent from the above example is that the manager has used a number of covert and arguably devious ploys in order to achieve his aim. Let us explore some of these in more detail, making particular reference to our definition.

Steven's motives were at best dubious or at worst dishonest, yet it is interesting to note how he structured Sue's expectations even before the meeting, by getting her to listen to the comments of another person. This can be a powerful influencing technique. Unfortunately in this example (like most of the other techniques used) it was applied in a negative manner. As a result of using these pre-meeting tactics, Steven had begun to prepare her to change her thinking.

During the meeting he deliberately gave vocal explicit support both to the programme and to her assertion of the importance of the venue. It was critical that he did this in order to be seen as 'whiter than white', acting only in the best interests of the company. The issue of the importance of the venue was then used against her.

In his meeting Steven used a variety of persuasive techniques including repetition, anxiety provocation and implicit coercion. While using these techniques he simultaneously continued to suggest a collaborative approach by using words like 'we'. Such behaviour gives conflicting messages and is inherently deceptive.

Steven achieves success by the use of a particularly subtle technique. He continued to increase Sue's anxiety by throwing a number of different issues at her (while not giving her time to respond) and when this was at its highest pitch, he offered her psychological relief by showing her a solution to her problem. This is accepted because he offers her a sweetener by which she can not only maintain her own self-esteem but also gain some additional kudos.

SOME ETHICAL ISSUES

The above case was fairly clear-cut. However, it might be suggested that some forms of manipulation are legitimate because the end justifies the means. This is not an argument to which we could subscribe.

In general terms many of us use techniques that might border on being manipulative. Where doubt exists then a useful framework as provided by our definition might be helpful. Alternatively we might consider our original definition of influencing: '**The process of getting other people to accept our view(s) and feel happy about it; and for them to remain persuaded and enthusiastic enough to influence positively other people.**'

People who regularly use techniques of manipulation to influence others will sometimes get away with it because they often choose easy targets, but in the long term other people tend to become wise to their style and treat them with extreme suspicion. Further, manipulative people are quite likely to find that other people will attempt to manipulate them, and a lot of time is therefore wasted playing games with one another.

So we are not advocating manipulation as an influencing style. Nevertheless we do recognize that we present a number of techniques below, which could be used in a manipulative way or in a positive influencing manner.

The important issue is the way in which such techniques are used. If we adopt a pull approach to influencing and follow the Model of Successful Influencing, then there will be an open discussion at the start regarding the objectives of both parties and the aim will be to achieve a result which leaves the dignity of all concerned intact. We would argue that one can use persuasive techniques in order to progress and speed the process of persuasion, but as previously described manipulation should be avoided.

THINKING ABOUT **PERSUASION**

It is important to recognize that the process of persuasion takes place in the other person's mind and that our role as successful influencer is to help the other person towards making a decision or taking positive action. In order to be able to achieve this we must have a clear understanding as to what we want the other person to know or do.

When presenting a persuasive argument there are essentially two approaches that might be taken: an appeal to logic or an appeal to emotion. It is quite common to see emotional arguments taken in advertising. For instance, when trying to persuade people to give to charity, a picture of starving children or suffering families may be shown, and this evokes emotions. The aim is to encourage you to write out a cheque there and then. While emotional arguments can be very effective the danger is that they persuade you in the short but not in the long term. So in the example above, while you might give to charity there and then, based on the emotional argument, you are less likely to be influenced to give on a regular basis.

Storyboard: The impact of fear

Chris was driving along at about 160 km per hour when he saw the carnage of a car crash on the roadway. Several vehicles were involved. It looked as if there were fatalities. After passing the accident he found that his speed seemed to slow naturally to about 120 km per hour.

This apparent change in his behaviour was probably the result of him seeing what had taken place and then having been suitably shocked, thinking along the lines of 'Oh, how awful, they were probably driving too fast – it's dangerous – I must start driving more slowly myself.' He drove more slowly for about the next hour and then gradually his speed crept back up to the normal level for fast driving.

As the above example suggests, fear is a very powerful emotion, yet unfortunately it does not last. Over time it dissipates and to be effective needs to be continuously reinforced. Hence coercion using emotional arguments is not necessarily a good influencing strategy.

In contrast, the logical approach tends to emphasize the importance of doing something because it makes sense on a rational basis. If the intention in influencing is to bring about a lasting change, then a logical approach to persuasion is likely to be more successful. Having said that, a logical process delivered with strong emotional tones will probably be better than a single-dimensional approach.

Let us move on to considering the two stages of **possibilities** and **preferences** before exploring the competences in depth.

POSSIBILITIES

In presenting a range of possibilities, a particularly persuasive approach is to include the proposals that you intend to make but to add them to a range of other possibilities. You may have a range of desired outcomes and it can be beneficial to include as possibilities your second and third choice outcomes. If you do not achieve your ideal outcome, then it may be that there are other options which would be more acceptable to you than no action at all. It is worth stating that one possibility is to do nothing; the thinking here is that you are showing, in what seems an objective way, that you have considered the full range of options. You might, though, summarize what you feel the implications of doing nothing are; they may appear so unacceptable that some action is bound to be taken.

The order in which you state the possibilities is significant. There is a natural perceptual distortion which means that we tend to pay particular attention to the early part and the final part of a presentation or discussion, often referred to as the primacy and recency effects. So if you state the possibility which you would like to see as the outcome first or last in your list of possibilities then this is likely to make more of an impact on the person you are attempting to persuade. A useful technique is to place your first choice first on the list of possibilities and your second choice last on the list.

Enumerating possibilities is not about a heavy sell; it is primarily to enable you to show your breadth of thinking about the subject and to structure the other person's expectations in readiness for your suggestions. Consequently it is important that the other person acknowledges that the list of possibilities is complete.

During the course of presenting possibilities it is important that you use the skills of building personal credibility and verbal persuasion.

BUILDING CREDIBILITY

It is wrong to try to give the other person the impression that we are good at everything. In the eyes of the other person this is too good to be true and will often be rejected; but at all costs avoid showing nervousness.

Building credibility is a prerequisite for getting someone easily to accept our point of view. It can be done in a number of ways but an important principle is to build credibility slowly and over time rather than with one enormous effort. Indeed, there is evidence to suggest that when we build credibility too quickly it can cause an adverse reaction.

Listed below are some of the common ways for building credibility:

- making passing reference to past successful projects or assignments;
- using a respected third-party name;
- discussing common acquaintances;
- discussing strengths modestly, ensuring that we acknowledge some weaknesses but positioning them in such a way that they might appear as strengths;
- showing how up-to-date you are on a subject;
- using real-life examples of success (taking care not to betray confidences);
- recognizing and publicly stating what you cannot discuss;
- speaking emphatically.

By contrast, avoid exaggerating or telling unbelievable stories. In addition, many fail because they show doubt and uncertainty in either their verbal or non-verbal behaviour.

PROPOSALS

Having discussed a range of possibilities, it is necessary to make proposals about further action. One should have a clear idea in advance of the meeting which proposals might be made; the secret, however, is to remain flexible about specific proposals because the discussion may reveal that the other person is cautious about certain possibilities and enthusiastic about others. When stated, proposals should be clear, concise and to the point. After stating them, we should pause for effect and to gain some feedback.

PAUSE FOR **THOUGHT**

1. *What does manipulation mean to you?*
2. *Which persuasive techniques do you feel you use well?*
3. *Which areas could you improve?*

INTEGRATING THE **COMPETENCIES**

In working through the techniques of persuasion, it is essential to view the process as dynamic and interactive. The model can help in giving structure and in serving as a checklist as different stages are completed, but there is a danger in allowing yourself to be constrained by it. If the other person wants to raise a 'put-off' early on in the discussion, then you will have to deal with this as it arises, which requires the secondary competence of adaptability.

If the discussion is with one other person or even a small team, then it is likely to be interactive and comprise a series of questions, answers and comments from all sides. If someone is attempting to persuade in a larger group, then there is necessarily more formality and the use of persuasive techniques might provide structure in the more formal discussion.

Questioning can ensure a sound understanding of the other person's viewpoint and perspective. In addition, specific types of question can be used in the persuasive dialogue actively to influence the other person.

The rhetorical question

This is a question to which a substantial answer is not expected. In a persuasive sense, rhetorical questions are often asked in a leading way. The intention is to lead the other person to answer in a particular way. The answer is either obvious or leads the person being persuaded down a particular path which the questioner has determined. Examples of rhetorical or leading questions are listed below with comments in brackets about where the questioner is trying to lead the person being persuaded.

- 'Do you believe quality is an important issue in your organization?'
  (Quality is important in most organizations so the answer is likely to be 'yes'; this question could be leading the respondent towards the acceptance of a proposed product or service which arguably will contribute to the improvement of quality in the business.)
- 'Are you interested in developing your own personal skills for the future?'

(Most people are interested in personally improving themselves; this question could be leading to a proposal of training or some sort of change in working practice.)
- 'Would you be interested in reducing your overhead costs?'
(Most people would be; this could be leading to the offer of a service, product or new working method.)

Rhetorical questions can be powerful if used with discretion. As with most persuasive techniques, they can backfire if used in the wrong context or in a very transparent way. The skill of the person trying to persuade is to be able to integrate such skills into a repertoire of behaviours and to apply judgement in their application.

The alternative closed question

With the alternative closed question the persuader offers the other person a choice, but a restricting one. A good example of this is where the parent, in trying to persuade the child to go to bed, asks, 'Would you like to put on your blue or green pyjamas?' The decision has already been made; the child has no choice but to get ready for bed. In a more subtle way, we often note such questions being used as a way of pressing for some action on the part of the other person. Another example of an alternative closed question is that used by the manager concerned to secure a second meeting with a colleague who is showing signs of resistance. She might say, 'Would you prefer me to come back for a further discussion tomorrow or would next week be better?'

The alternative closed question can be a very effective way of moving things forward if there seems to be a lack of action and if the person you are trying to persuade seems to be prevaricating. The important skill is to be able to judge whether the other person is close to accepting a proposition and then to use the alternative closed question. Such judgements can only be made after considering all the verbal and non-verbal signals. If this is misjudged and the question used at too early a stage, then the other person may consider the technique manipulative and resent it.

Assumption statements

A similar approach, which is often used effectively, is to use an assumed closed comment or assumption statement. This is the verbal technique of making a comment that implies the other person is going to take the preferred course of action. Using the above example of the manager who is trying to persuade a colleague to meet again in the future, an assumed closed comment would be: 'When we meet again, I propose we ask some of your team into the meeting to help them understand what we're discussing.' The issue here is not so much one of involving the colleague's team members as getting the colleague to attend a meeting. By moving one step ahead of the next move, there is an implication that the meeting is bound to take place.

CONTINUING TO MAKE AN **IMPACT**

Impressions management is about other people forming opinions of us, which will be influenced by their perceptual processes.

Managing the first impression

We stress the importance of first impressions and their contribution to the primacy effect, a common perceptual distortion resulting from our strong tendency to make judgements based on an assessment made in the first four minutes of meeting someone. It is fundamental to the success or otherwise of making impact and building rapport.

First impressions could prove to be accurate or conversely they could be erroneous. The key issue from an influencing point of view is to recognize the importance of making the impression that we want to make right from the start, because it is very difficult to change the other person's perception once an impression has been formed. We use the term 'impressions management' to describe the way that one should recognize and attempt to influence the other person's impression.

Apart from the phenomenon of first impressions, there are a number of ways in which impressions tend to be distorted, and these provide further opportunities to influence others. Such an area, the flip side of first impressions, is described by way of the 'recency effect', which shows that last impressions are also of particular importance. In the same way that people naturally place an overemphasis on the first period in an interaction, so do they tend to focus particularly on the most recent contact.

Using recency

One area in which we see the recency effect most clearly is that of performance review. If attempting to review the performance of a subordinate over a period of, say, one year, the tendency is to review only the last few months. If one is attempting to influence someone then there may be opportunities to use the recency effect in a positive way. For instance: if making a formal presentation, it is important to have a powerful conclusion; or, if you are due shortly to meet a potential client whom you are concerned to impress, you might send him or her a relevant article or paper which supports your main message. In doing this, when you do meet, the potential client is likely to recall the recent article and, if this has made a positive impact, recency is likely to work in your favour.

Stereotyping ourselves and others

Humans have a tendency to stereotype other people; we figuratively put them into boxes or label them and say that, because someone is 'x', he or she is bound also to have 'y' qualities. To try to make judgements about people, we try to make them fit into a stereotype or even a number of stereotypes based for instance on gender, race, profession, social class or age. The reason that we tend to stereotype others is that it is convenient, and provides a quick and easy way of making judgements about others when we do not have the time or inclination to get to know what the individual is really like. In terms of making accurate judgements about people, there are dangers in stereotyping: first, there is a possibility of getting it wrong; and second, if the person you are stereotyping becomes aware of it, he or she will quite likely feel insulted. So from an influencing perspective, stereotyping other people is unhelpful. It is interesting though to note the extent to which humour is based on stereotypes.

But let's take a look at stereotyping from another perspective. Whether you like it or not, other people stereotype you all the time. They will form stereotypes based on minor amounts of information such as your name and your role. When they do meet you, the stereotyping process will continue based on, for instance, your looks, dress and the way you speak. They will even form stereotypes based on the accessories you wear and with which you surround yourself.

Some people will, in a fairly obvious way, attempt to make a statement about themselves by adorning their bodies and surroundings with accessory symbols. After all, who wears a Rolex watch in order to be able to tell the time? Such accessories are about making a statement regarding one's worth or values. And this applies not only to material wealth. Consider, for instance, the sportsperson who wears a tie or scarf with the club colours or motif displayed. The message here could be 'I am sporty' or 'I am a team person' or even 'I am a member of an exclusive organization'. In this example, it could also be a way of showing identification with like-minded people.

In order to influence the stereotypes which others form of you, it is important to ask the question 'What is the stereotype that this person may have of me and do I want to reinforce it or do I want to shatter it?'

PAUSE FOR **THOUGHT**

1. *Consider the stereotypes other people are likely to hold of you. What generalizations are they likely to make based on your: appearance, age, job, culture, speech, background, education, interests, family, location, car, accessory symbols?*
2. *Now consider an influencing situation in which you are likely to find yourself in the near future. How appropriate are the stereotypes which might be held of you? Do they actually help you influence or do they hinder your influencing position?*
3. *Next, consider how you might reinforce relevant stereotypes and how you might shatter inappropriate ones.*

Halo or horns

Another major perceptual distortion to which thought must be given in impressions management is the 'halo and horns' effect. Again there is a natural human tendency to put a figurative halo or alternatively a set of horns over another person's head because of just one of their strengths or weaknesses.

An example of the halo effect is recruiting someone for a job as marketing manager because he or she once played international sport; sporting prowess has no relationship with marketing skill but a false linkage has been made between the two issues. Similarly it could be that, because of one negative factor, an assumption is made that everything a certain person will ever do is bound to result in failure. For instance, if assessing a member of your team for suitability to work on a high-profile client contract, an assumption might be made that because there were some problems with one client in the past, he or she is bound to have similar problems in the future and is therefore ruled out.

From an impressions management perspective, the important point is to recognize that the phenomenon can affect the qualities other people attribute to you. If you are able to identify the nature or source of the halo or horns, then you can encourage the halo effect and discourage the horns. As long as this is done in such a way that there is no dishonest intent, which would suggest manipulation, then reinforcing positive haloes can prove an effective influencing technique. Of course you need the confidence to be able to live up to the positive image others have of you, and if you feel there is evidence of an entirely misplaced halo effect, then the best approach is to explain the limits of your knowledge or expertise. With the horns effect, it is important to challenge and confront comments that may be unfounded. We will look later at the subject of how to confront assertively.

VERBAL **PERSUASION**

Having considered a number of ways that one can use perceptual distortion to manage the impressions others form of us, we will now discuss some of the practical techniques that can help the process of persuasion. These techniques are drawn from our studies of the specific behaviours of successful and persuasive international figures who in many ways can serve as effective role models.

Build personal credibility slowly

It has been observed that some of the most persuasive figures and speakers are subtle in building their own credibility. They will tend to build up their own images gradually and steadily. Often they do this through low-key, almost passing, references to their own relevant experience or expertise. They will not be afraid to discuss their own strengths and abilities but will do so without overselling themselves. So a manager, in building credibility with a customer, might start by referring to her current senior role and a little later would mention in passing some of the organizations she has worked for during her career, being careful to select those organizations from her portfolio to which the customer is likely to relate best. She might at a later stage mention her role in developing certain well-known products and later again refer to articles she has had published in relevant industry journals.

This approach is quite different from that taken by people who naïvely believe the best way to persuade people as to their credibility is to declare all their strengths upfront at the start of the interaction. This approach can be seen as rather too forceful and other people are prone to back off at this hard-sell approach.

Identification

Successful influencers are able to identify well with other people; they are able to give the impression that they are similar to the other person. They are very skilled in quickly picking up and building on relevant information about possible areas of common interest; they will not be afraid openly to discuss common interests, and they will give the impression that, because of them, there is a unique relationship. This process of identification tends to accelerate the building of trust and the feeling that there is some common bond. Judgement needs to be used when applying this technique; it can, for instance, be a dangerous strategy to attempt to identify by referring to a common interest which you cannot support if the other person decides to probe with deeper discussion. But approaches to identification could be as simple as:

- identifying the areas that you both have in common and making sure these similarities are known;
- asking about the other person's children and talking about yours if they are of a similar age;
- referring to people you both know personally;
- showing similar experiences.

One particular method of identifying with the other person is through the use of third-party references. By referring, for example, to the work being carried out with a customer in the same industry as the potential client, a salesperson is able implicitly to demonstrate an understanding of the client's business as well as demonstrating that he is valued by others.

On a cautionary note: as we previously mentioned, discussing family or using self-disclosure may be culturally unacceptable in some societies.

Painting pictures

Consider for a moment what goes on in your head when you think. Do you think in words, images, pictures, faces or situations? Do you think in colour or black-and-white? Most people to whom we ask this question have to think about it quite hard. The majority say that they think in pictures or images; some even explain that when they think they almost see a film screen with scenes being acted out in their mind. Only rarely do people say that when they think, they see text or numbers.

Bearing this in mind, there is a lot to be said for attempting to create pictures and images in the mind of the other person when trying to persuade them. It is particularly advantageous if you can create a picture of how things could be if your proposals were accepted. In this sense the use of metaphors and analogies can be very powerful. Consider the images conjured up by the following statements: 'Bringing about major culture change in the organization is difficult. It is rather like trying to turn a super-tanker in the ocean – you have to accept it won't happen overnight, but once you do get things moving it will be hard to stop'; and 'He is so tenacious. He is like a terrier dog constantly snapping at your heels to try and get information out of you. He is so persistent that eventually you give in and let him have his way.'

Some people seem to have a natural ability to paint pictures, which gives them an advantage when it comes to influencing others. A related verbal technique to increase impact is the use of alliteration, as in the title to this section, 'Painting pictures', which uses alliteration to aid recall as well as conjuring up a visual image.

Selective head nods

When two people have established a strong rapport, then it is common to see them subconsciously mimicking each other's non-verbal behaviour. It is possible to use this information consciously and to encourage the other person to mimic you. In an influencing situation where you are attempting to gain agreement to a proposal, if you selectively nod your head, frequently you will notice that the other person also starts nodding. This may be an effective approach to gaining agreement as studies into body language have shown that, when a person is forced into using a particular non-verbal gesture, the relevant thinking follows. So experiments where certain members of the audience in a presentation were instructed to keep their arms folded have shown that their learning was significantly reduced compared to those who were allowed to sit as they pleased. If a person starts to mimic your selective head nods, then he or she is more likely to agree to your proposition than if not engaging in such mimicry.

Repeat, repeat, repeat

The benefits of repetition in persuading other people should not be under-estimated. The process of using the same words ensures that key messages are reinforced. This is an approach that some politicians and public speakers use strongly. Repetition can also help in buying thinking-time for the speaker.

One approach to repetition is to use certain words at the end of a sentence and then, after a suitable pause, start the next sentence with the same words or expression. For example: 'The main reason we should mobilize our forces is because of the external threat. . . The external threat is so powerful because. . .'.

Emotional stimulation

It has been recognized in the marketing field for some time that one way of increasing the demand for your product or service is to appeal to the potential purchaser's emotions. Some advertisers have capitalized on this in quite an aggressive way. Consider the many advertisements for motor cars that tell a romantic story of boy-meets-girl, or the up-market ice-cream advertisements which manage to give erotic connotations to the product. Such approaches have sometimes proved controversial; for instance, in the area of cigarette sales, linking the product with sporty, macho or romantic images has led to accusations of exploitation.

The learning-point from the marketeers is that, if we can appeal to the other person's emotions (particularly pleasure, joy and happiness), then there is more chance of gaining interest in what we are proposing. Consequently if we can make our idea sound fun, exciting or interesting, there is significantly more likelihood that it will be accepted than if we simply propose the facts in a dry manner.

Psychological relief

In some ways this is the opposite of emotional stimulation. There are many advertisements that work by generating fear in a person, and then proposing a way of relieving the fear. So, for instance, cosmetics are often sold on the basis that they will relieve you of the potential implications of ageing. You might be encouraged to fit a fire alarm in your home after you have seen the frightening pictures of a family sleeping while their house is burning down. In a similar vein, consider this example of an extract from a letter from a financial services organization selling its insurance products to the self-employed.

Storyboard: Victims and rescuers

Dear Mr X,

Did you know that in this country 10 per cent of men over the age of 40 suffer from long-term sickness of at least one year's duration? Half of all family breadwinners are forced to retire early through sickness and the majority of these are left unable to provide adequately for their families. Furthermore, with reductions in the amount of state aid available, there is a serious danger of being left to face a future of poverty.

With our new family income protection policy, however, it is possible to provide for your family's future in the unfortunate event of. . .

The above example was not particularly subtle, yet we discovered that this kind of approach produces a better than average response rate.

In an influencing context, it is possible to sense when the person you are attempting to persuade is feeling under some pressure from a problem which you may be able to relieve. For instance, you may be attempting to persuade your boss to allow you to take on more responsibility in your job role. Using this approach, you could spend some time making sure it is realized there is a lot of extra administrative work building up and that it must be placing quite a pressure on the boss. Having built up the pressure psychologically, you would then relieve it by offering your assistance. In this example your boss would feel only too pleased to delegate or hand over certain tasks to you in order to relieve the pressure on him or herself. So occasionally the tactical raising of the temperature can create a climate which is conducive to raising the demand for your assistance.

Appealing to status

It is well known in the area of sales that one sure way of creating demand from a potential customer is to make him or her feel important. If you can present your product or service in such a way that it suggests the customer's image will be enhanced in the eyes of other people, then he or she is much more likely to respond in a positive way.

Take for instance the salesperson who identifies his customer as a young upwardly mobile professional and appeals to status by saying, 'This is a beautiful car. The thing about driving a BMW is that it really makes a statement to other people that you have arrived in life!' This may sound like a rather obvious, unsubtle approach; however, there is no doubt that some people are particularly motivated by recognition and status. On a more subtle level is the manager who delegates a task to her subordinate while implying that, if it is carried out successfully, it will raise the profile of the subordinate amongst her superiors.

In terms of motivation theory, if the technique of offering psychological relief appeals to our human need for security and safety, then the technique of appealing to status capitalizes on the human requirement for recognition and acceptance by others. One needs to exercise some caution in appealing to the status of the other person; if the technique is overdone it can appear as flattery, which may work occasionally but if overused can seem transparent and manipulative.

Linked to this approach is the technique of persuading people by suggesting that what you have to offer is in high demand or is what other people want. If you are able to suggest that the demand is coming from a person or organization respected by the person you are attempting to persuade, then you are likely to increase still further the level of demand.

Have you ever had the experience of deciding to buy something and when you come to order you are informed that the product is in short supply because of high demand? This usually increases individual demand dramatically. Of course some people have used this understanding of human psychology in a coercive way: take for instance the estate agent who, when you place an offer on your dream property, informs you that there is another potential buyer in the race. This ploy might be used in order to encourage you to increase the level of your offer so that you can secure the property. Yet it can also easily backfire!

In influencing situations generally it is possible to use the same sort of approach to encourage others to accept your proposals. It could be, for instance, that you convince your boss of the need to upgrade the departmental computing facilities by referring to how other successful managers in the organization have made similar changes. This might capitalize on your boss being interested in having what others have, as well as on others who have made the upgrade being of senior status.

So far in this chapter, we have considered building personal credibility and verbal persuasion. A critical component of verbal persuasion is concerned not with what we say but with how we say it. Diction is concerned with the clarity with which we say something. Generally speaking, we found that successful influencers did not necessarily have an extended vocabulary yet their diction was almost always clear and precise. They appeared to be conscious of creating the words they were using by the movements of their mouths. In particular they would often emphasize specific words or syllables. Vocabulary does not appear to be a critical issue of influencing, yet influencers do appear to select their words with care. By contrast, the less effective influencers tended to use more hesitant words or expressions, riddled with doubt and uncertainty.

How often have we heard the expression 'It's not what you say, it's the way that you say it'? Although we would argue that this is a somewhat simplistic way of looking at things, we do believe that the way we use our voices can be significant in influencing others. Consequently we feel that this is an important secondary competence of influence.

One of the most surprising findings was that successful influencers are very flexible in their style and speed of delivery. Overall there was a tendency to talk slightly more quickly than the average, and what was interesting was that as the number of words per minute increased, the other person was able to hear more than if the speaker had been speaking at an average rate.

We also found that successful influencers appeared to have good control of their facility to slow the voice down. This latter aspect seemed to have a positive effect on their audience who, when the voice slowed down (and frequently also became quieter), seemed to increase their level of attention. In general terms the volume appeared to be just a little louder than that which was required for the occasion. These individuals would use the full tone of their voices and then they would often contrast it with a pause or quiet level of speaking. People with voices naturally deeper than average tended to find it easier to have others listen to them. By contrast, some higher voices are believed to be better at portraying emotion or enthusiasm.

To summarize, the way in which we use our voices can do things that either enhance our message or detract from it.

Focused feedback

Arguably the most powerful technique of persuasion is that of providing focused feedback. In an influencing situation it is often necessary to be able to let the person we are dealing with know how effectively he or she is operating and to inform of the impact being made on you or on others.

Focused feedback is about the ability to provide others with feedback in such a way that they are influenced to make changes in the way they operate. If feedback is given in such a way that it is accepted and the other person on reflection decides to make changes in the future, then such feedback may be considered effective.

Focused feedback is the ability to provide feedback by being specific, descriptive and non-evaluative and by focusing on modifiable behaviours. Such feedback is given in a timely way and is balanced. It is for the benefit of the recipient, not the provider.

PAUSE FOR **THOUGHT**

1. *When did you last give somebody some positive feedback?*
2. *What was the impact on him or her?*
3. *Do you always follow the above guidelines on giving feedback?*
4. *What aspects of your verbal skills in influencing can you improve?*
5. *Do you need to speak more loudly in order to command attention?*

What is the use of providing some supposed feedback to someone if he or she is incapable of making the changes you would like to see? Or what if, as is often the case, the feedback is provided months after the event to which it is meant to relate? Feedback is sometimes given so that the person giving it feels better; this is particularly the case with feedback of a negative nature. This is not focused feedback and probably does little to influence the other person.

It is interesting to note that feedback often has negative connotations. Consider the situation where the boss calls the subordinate on a Friday afternoon and says, 'Can you come and see me on Monday morning? I would like to give you some feedback.' Such a comment is guaranteed to spoil the weekend for the subordinate, who will be preoccupied with wondering, 'What have I done wrong?' Similarly, consider the comment made by the businessman or woman who says to a colleague staying at the same hotel, 'I am going to go down to the reception desk and give them some real feedback.' The statements in these examples are clearly loaded and imply that there is likely to be a strongly negative flavour to the discussion. All too often the word 'feedback' is used to signify a release of emotion on the part of the giver of the feedback, rather than being seen as the provision of useful information for the receiver.

We would do well to remember the concept of feedback in an engineering sense. A feedback loop is a built-in mechanism in systems to provide information on performance so that changes can be made in order for the system to continue to operate effectively. In a human sense there is no reason why the same interpretation should not apply. Feedback need not always be associated with letting someone know where he or she has got it wrong; it is also extremely helpful to let people know when and how they managed to get it right so that they can continue to do so in the future.

In order to influence the behaviour of another person there are a number of useful ground rules which will help to ensure the feedback is effective. First of all, feedback should describe the behaviour observed. There is no need to make value judgements and personal comments such as 'You are hopeless' or 'You are great.' This sort of comment does little to inform the other person why you considered him or her to be hopeless or great. Without this specific knowledge, it is difficult to reinforce strengths and minimize weaknesses. So if, for instance, you are providing feedback to a colleague on his or her contribution to a meeting, a descriptive piece of feedback might be given as follows: 'I believe you showed real strengths in that meeting. First of all, you were one of the early speakers, which meant that people paid attention to your inputs throughout. Second, you used some powerful examples to highlight your opinions. OK, you might have spent a little more time listening to Brian and some of the quiet members of the team, but overall I have to admire your meeting skills.'

If we analyse this brief piece of feedback, we notice that by saying 'I believe' it is presented as just one person's opinion or interpretation rather than a definitive and omniscient judgement which could appear arrogant. Two specific strengths are described, the early contribution and the use of examples. This tells the person what to do again in the future. One area for improvement is presented but it is not laboured and it is descriptive, providing a specific example of what might be done differently next time, which is listening to all members of the team.

It is also important when providing feedback to others that it is given soon after the event to which it relates. It would be of little value, for example, giving the feedback about the meeting in the above illustration several meetings later; the impact and relevance of the feedback would be lost.

The amount of judgement which is provided is a matter of fine judgement. Too much and the other person will reach saturation point when he or she may appear to be listening but information is not being interpreted. When providing feedback on another person's behaviour, just two or three specific examples to back up a description of an observed behaviour are sufficient, and in an informal discussion it would be unrealistic to cover more than, say, three different behaviours.

When feedback is provided it should be given with the implied message, 'Take it or leave it', because it is not possible to force a person to accept feedback about personal issues. One's own self-perception will always be distorted because of the psychological defence mechanisms we use to protect our egos. Providing feedback is a way of attempting to give people the opportunity to develop realistic images of themselves. If they receive similar feedback from a number of different people, then they are more likely to accept it as valid.

The other rule in giving feedback is to try to focus on behaviours which are modifiable. In an obvious example, there is little to be gained from providing feedback to a presenter that he or she is 'six inches too short in height to make an impact'; advice about making an impact might better be directed at developing impact through voice projection and the content of the presentation.

Finally, feedback should always be balanced. In the above example, strengths and also weaknesses are identified. It is worth considering that in matters relating to personal and behavioural style, a person's strengths and weaknesses can always be related. Feedback is more likely to be accepted if it identifies both strengths and weaknesses. Furthermore, if it can be presented as a 'feedback sandwich' with strengths-weaknesses-strengths being covered in this order, then it is likely to be more palatable. You might at this stage be wondering, 'How can all weaknesses be related to strengths?'

If so, consider the following list of strengths and potentially corresponding weaknesses in Table 6.1.

When considered in this way, it is not difficult to find strengths related to weaknesses or areas for development. We are not saying that one must always try to say 'nice things' when giving feedback, but when discussing personality-related behaviours it is important to recognize the richness and complexity of human personality and to look for strengths as well as weaknesses. If this proves difficult, then the positive note might simply relate to the behaviours or new approaches to which the person commits in the future.

In the workplace we are seeing a significant broadening in the use of feedback as an influencing skill. The successful influencers we have observed through our research consistently showed strong ability to provide feedback to others, and to confront and provide such feedback in a way that was likely to help the other person recognize the need for change.

POSITIVE **ACTION**

This is in many ways the most important but also the most neglected of the stages of the Model of Successful Influencing. All too often good persuasive skills are demonstrated but there is a failure to agree what will happen next.

Table 6.1 Strengths and weaknesses

Strengths	Weaknesses
Competitive, strong-willed, task-oriented	Overbearing, domineering, autocratic
Influential, strong social skills, good at making impact	Superficial, lacking depth or substance
Reliable, neighbourly, steady	Unexciting, uncomfortable with change
Good with detail, procedures and rules	Non risk-taker, unadventurous uncomfortable with uncertainty
Reflective, thoughtful, pensive, intelligent, probing	Hesitant, withdrawn, introverted
Conceptual, strategic visionary	Daydreamer, head in the clouds, not practical

How often have you attended a meeting and found that the various parties leave the meeting with different pictures of what has been agreed?

Often the failure to 'ask for the order' is influenced by a fear of being seen as over-pushy or aggressive. However, this stage need not be conducted in a 'hard sell' style. It can be as straightforward as summarizing who has committed to do what or even putting a date in the diary for the next meeting.

Another common reason for failing to be successful at this stage is our fear of rejection. The only way we can manage this is by positive inner dialogues and by realizing that saying 'no' is often a signal for saying, 'I am not yet convinced.' In situations like this the secondary competence of tenacity becomes paramount. This is about our ability to keep at something when it could be easier to concede or give up. This competence is linked to our skills of judgement, as we need to recognize when it is better to give up.

We have considered how to introduce possibilities effectively, we have explored persuasion and we have highlighted the need to convert persuasive success into action. We now turn our attention to the issue of non-verbal communication.

seven

NON-VERBAL
COMMUNICATION

In this chapter we:

- explain the importance of the signs and signals of body language as the critical component of communication;
- consider the impact of our own non-verbal behaviour on other people;
- explore the need to ensure our body language is consistent with our verbal message;
- look further at the technique of mirroring;
- explore the subject of cultural differences and body language.

INTRODUCTION

Arguably non-verbal behaviour or body language is our original language; that is to say, in the history of mankind our use of language is a relatively new feature of our communication. Indeed, it is assumed that prehistoric man communicated mostly by signs and signals interspersed with different kinds of grunting noise. We digress from the process stages in the Model of Successful Influencing in order to cover this fundamental area of communication. Non-verbals play a part in all our face-to-face influencing; indeed, evidence suggests that the majority content of your message is received by the listener via your body language, hence our desire to give this subject its own chapter.

In this chapter we are going to discuss the importance of non-verbal communication with a particular focus on how it relates to the influencing situation. We will consider specifically how one can interpret the body language of others, obtaining an accurate picture of their feelings, and how conversely it is possible to use one's own body language to add weight to our verbal influencing abilities.

Body language is one area where we are frequently asked for the definitive interpretation of a particular gesture or behaviour. This we feel is an inappropriate approach to the whole subject because, for instance, if we take the example of trying to interpret what it means when someone crosses his or her arms, this gesture in isolation could give clues to a number of possible feelings. It could be that the person:

■ is being defensive;
■ is making him or herself comfortable;
■ is nursing a sore elbow;
■ has cold hands.

This example is given in order to highlight the danger of looking at one aspect of body language and trying to put a label on it. A more reliable, though not infallible, approach is to seek to identify what we call 'clusters' of behaviour. We will consider some of the important clusters of behaviour to look out for when interpreting the body language of the person you are trying to influence. We will also discuss the importance of ensuring you demonstrate effective body language that is compatible with the verbal message you are conveying.

THE RELEVANCE OF BODY **LANGUAGE**

The significance of non-verbal communication in communicating an influential message cannot be underestimated. A number of studies of the relative importance of words and behaviours in making impact or imparting understanding have been made. Among these findings are those of Albert Mehrabian (1971) who found that only 7 per cent of the impact came from spoken words, 38 per cent from intonation and 55 per cent from non-verbal communication: see Figure 7.1.

These statistics may seem surprising; however, have you ever had the experience of listening to someone say what is probably the right thing to say but feeling that he or she does not mean it? It could be the waitress who says 'Enjoy your meal' while looking over to the next table and sounding as though she has said the same thing a thousand times already that day; or the team member who, when you ask if your instruction has been understood, says with a quivering voice, 'Yes, I understand what you are saying', while looking down and frowning in a confused way.

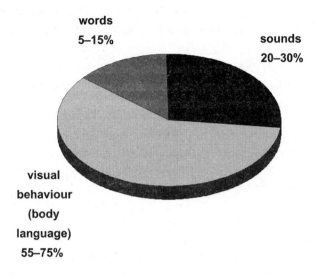

words
5–15%

sounds
20–30%

visual
behaviour
(body
language)
55–75%

Figure 7.1 Understanding in face-to-face communication

If these examples sound familiar it is likely that the reason you doubted the spoken word, even though the right verbal messages were provided, was because you intuitively interpreted the non-verbal communication. The non-verbal channel's power can be seen if you study the communication process when the opportunity to observe the other person visually is removed. Take, for example, the telephone as a means of communication. Here one has no choice but to rely on the words and the intonation or tone of voice. It is interesting that telephone sales people and telephone receptionists are often trained to smile when they speak to the customer by telephone; the implication is that the smile will reflect in the tone of voice, which will make a positive impact on the other person.

If you have ever tried to give someone directions by telephone, you may have found yourself with the handset balanced between your shoulder and ear while you wave your hands about to help you to visualize the roads and turnings. This example shows the importance of non-verbal communication in helping the speaker to express him or herself.

USING OUR **SPACE**

How close do you let other people get to you physically? If you reflect on this question you will probably recognize that this depends on a number of factors. To begin with, it is likely to depend on how well you know the person. If you know him or her in an intimate way, it is likely that you will allow them into your 'intimate zone', which could range from physical touch to an area half a metre away from you. Outside our intimate zone we also have a 'personal zone', which may be between half a metre and a metre around us; this is the distance at which we tend to operate when in friendly conversation with people with whom we feel comfortable, like our friends or close acquaintances.

Beyond this distance we have what can be considered the 'social zone'. This is usually between one and three and a half metres around us, and it is where we tend to operate with people we do not know very well. Finally there is the broader 'public zone', which we work in when in bigger or more formal groups, and which is any distance beyond our social zone.

To explore this idea of zones, try observing the way in which people select their seats on a partially empty train, or their place on a crowded beach. Usually each person will sit in a seat or space an equal distance from other people. Such behaviour is almost always unconscious. Another interesting example of how critical space is for individuals is to study what happens when another person invades our personal space such as on the underground or in a lift. People we do not know are forced into our intimate or personal zones. The usual response, if unable to distance ourselves physically, is to try at least to distance ourselves psychologically. Consequently we will look away trying desperately to avoid eye contact, studying advertisements intensely or staring at the floor indicator lights as though they have some deep meaning. In a similar way when you are in conversation with someone you know well, try moving away from him or her into the social rather than personal zone; it is likely that this will be noticed and an attempt made to close the gap.

As with many aspects of non-verbal behaviour, however, this matter of physical space is culturally affected. So, for example in a Latin or Middle Eastern culture, it may be normal and quite acceptable to stand physically close to the other person even if he or she is not well known, and it may even be acceptable to touch him or her. In British and some Northern European cultures, this approach may be considered far too familiar and more distance felt appropriate until the relationship is well established. Again, as with many of the cultural differences we have discussed it is advisable to recognize that differences exist and accept that others may not behave in the way that you would. It may feel uncomfortable to change one's own approach and to adopt the other person's approach, but it may be possible to modify one's behaviour.

Apart from the norms of physical space between people there are tactical considerations. Humans tend to be very territorial in their nature and often we see some interesting 'prowling' and 'staking out' of territory in the early part of a meeting. Leaning against objects, or sitting, or touching things, may signal 'I belong here.' In a similar way when a person is trying to establish a dominant position he or she may demonstrate the following types of behaviour:

■ talking down – holding the chin up and looking down at the other person, maybe using spectacles to achieve the same results;
■ turning the shoulders in the direction of the person, to suggest they are being ignored because they are not important enough to command attention;
■ crowding out – imposing oneself physically, leaning over or looking down at the other person;
■ putting something onto the other person's desk or territory;
■ sitting with feet on a desk, maybe while leaning back with hands behind the head.

These are quite aggressive techniques but some people do use them to establish early dominance. It can be quite amusing if you see two people both playing the same game. If someone else uses these techniques on you, you have essentially three choices: you could back off, do nothing or take the same approach. Backing off is a passive approach and will reinforce in the mind of the other person that you can be intimidated; this is more likely to lead him or her to intimidate you in other parts of the discussion. Not responding, but holding your ground, is likely to demonstrate that you are not prepared to be pushed around and may result in the other person dropping intimidating tactics. Using the same approach, meeting aggression with aggression, is a high-risk approach; the other person may react by backing off or the non-verbal conflict may escalate into more overt confrontation.

SEATING AND POSITION

The other territorial issue worthy of consideration relates to the physical surroundings and furniture layout. Consider this example. You enter the room and notice that the manager is at the top of a T-shaped desk. You have the choice of a chair near the door at the far end from your host, or a chair on the top desk on a diagonal from his or her chair. Where would you sit when invited to take a seat?

The room layout here is a 'power set-up'. The layout of the large desk with a row of tables running off from it to form a T-shape suggests that the manager is making a point right from the start, which is 'I am the boss, and people come to consult me as an authority'. If you select the furthest chair you are clearly putting yourself in a subservient position and it may be difficult to work on an equal basis. Conversely, if you select the chair on the top desk you are entering a more personal zone, and adopting more of a consulting position. This could be a high-risk strategy if the manager actually wants to keep a physical and psychological distance, or it could break down the barriers of formality right from the start. The importance of sitting positions and room layout should not be underestimated. In order to influence effectively it is necessary both to be aware of the messages we may be giving others and to interpret the messages they are giving us.

Below we list a number of commonly used seating arrangements together with situations where they may be appropriate or otherwise.

Directly opposite

Possible interpretation:	Confrontational
	Business-like
	Formal
When to use:	When seeking to tackle someone head on
When not to use:	When seeking to create rapport or break down barriers

Corner to corner

Possible interpretation:	Less formal
	Joint problem solving
	Equal footing
When to use:	When offering help or when trying to break the ice if the other person may be intimidated (eg an interview) and when there is a need for a writing surface
When not to use:	When it is important to establish that you are in charge or when you want to use an autocratic style

No barriers

Possible interpretation:	Informal
	Counselling
	Closeness
	Co-operative
	Could seem threatening as there is no barrier to 'hide' behind

When to use:	Counselling situations
	Side by side on car journeys, which
	tends to be a good position for
	listening and sharing information
When not to use:	When the other person may be
	expecting a more formal
	approach

Another interesting aspect of sitting positions is the way people sit in their chairs. One classic, if rather extreme sitting position is the 'chair straddle', where the person turns the chair around and sits so that the back of the seat forms a supposed armrest that is in fact a barrier behind which to hide and from which to take a superior or even aggressive position in the discussion. Another dimension of sitting positions is the extent to which people will make themselves seem bigger or smaller then they really are. This may sound rather absurd but the two extremes are the person who leans forward and sits upright, pushing the torso outwards, in order to show dominance and the person who shrinks back into the seat, hunching shoulders and looking downwards, in order to show submission or lack of confidence. The message here is that if you want to make a powerful point with impact then you need to look the part and sound the part even if this means dominating physically and raising your voice on occasions.

HONESTY AND **DECEIT**

In the neurological field there have been some fascinating studies on the subject of eye movements. It has been shown that if people are trying to remember a real event then they are likely to glance to the left as they use the right sides of their brain to recall a picture of the event. If, however, they are trying to create a situation in their minds, then they are more likely to look to the right. So if someone is making something up, or attempting to fabricate, then he or she is likely to look to the right in accessing the left side of the brain to assemble a logical argument. To test this you might like to observe the behaviour of leading politicians when you suspect they are being 'economical with the truth'; do they look to their right or to their left?

In addition, there are a number of other non-verbal signs which, when observed in clusters, could provide strong evidence that you are hearing something other than the entire truth. Being aware of this is clearly advantageous in influencing situations. Having identified that someone is not telling the truth is the first step; the next is to consider why he or she is reacting in such a way. The reasons could be numerous including:

■ fear of telling the truth and the effect it could have on you (consider whether you intimidate the person and whether with effective listening and questioning skills you could get to the real issues);

■ a passive approach and lack of ability to say 'no' (this is often linked to lack of ability to be assertive and we address this in the next chapter);

■ a feeling that he or she is being pressurized (consider whether you are taking too much of a 'push' as opposed to a 'pull' approach to influencing);

■ he or she is prone to fantasize and exaggerate (you are unlikely to change this trait because it is often used as a personal psychological defence mechanism, but it may be appropriate to challenge occasionally);

■ reasons outside his or her control, often to do with organizational politics, which mean that he or she is unable to tell the truth at this stage (it may be best to be patient or to confront the issue of other influences in play);

■ he or she is trying to influence you in a forceful or coercive way (challenge the approach directly by stating that you recognize you are being coerced, and question whether this is the sort of person or organization you should be dealing with).

The key to identifying if someone may be withholding information or not telling the truth is to look for lack of consistency between the verbal message and the non-verbal communication. The reason that this approach is so reliable is because it is quite possible for someone to lie verbally but it is extremely difficult, almost impossible, to deceive over a period of time with one's body language.

Have you ever watched a play or film and said, 'That actor is unconvincing?' If so it is likely that what you detected was a lack of consistency between the verbal and non-verbal components of the message being communicated. Often what differentiates a brilliant actor from a mediocre one is the ability to match verbal messages with effective use of clusters of non-verbal communication.

We now explore non-verbals using a storyboard.

Storyboard: Things are not necessarily all they appear to be

Patrick was unhappy; the negotiations had not gone exactly the way he had anticipated. In part he felt his client had not really listened to what he was saying. Now it seemed that he was going to have to concede on the issue of improved delivery to ensure that he could meet their mid-December deadline.

He pushed his chair back from the table, sat back and closed his notebook (**withdrawn**). 'Of course it's not a problem for us,' he said, his eyes looking down at the floor (**being evasive**). 'I said before we can meet any delivery times to fit in with your needs.'

His client went on to explain how they were re-scheduling their production on the new line and how this new schedule would really help them manage their inventory and costs better.

Patrick fidgeted in his chair. His arms and legs were crossed (**defensive**) but he forced himself to smile and look interested. It was noticeable though how he was unable to maintain eye contact. His hands played alternately with the end of his tie and the ring on his finger (**anxiety**).

He suddenly had an idea. He sat up, raised his hand as if to speak (**keen**) and said, 'If we were able to increase your stock holdings without you incurring additional costs, would you be able to maintain the existing production schedule?'

His client moved forward, adopting a similar body posture (**interest**). 'Tell me more.' Patrick went on to explain his proposal. He noticed that as his client was listening his head was slightly inclined (**listening**). Similarly he saw that the client was nodding his head in agreement. As he noticed the client's behaviour, he suddenly became aware that he too was nodding his head (**encouraging agreement**) although it was he who was doing the talking.

He moved closer still, yet his voice got quieter as his persuasive style continued. His client pulled away slightly, which worried him; however, the smile and response of 'Good, good, excellent' reassured him that he was turning things around.

In the above example, Patrick allows his negative behaviour to reflect his disappointment that the negotiations are not going his way. After initially pulling away from the client, he exacerbated the situation by showing anxiety through playing with his tie and the ring on his finger. However, he did pull it around, using both mirroring and mimicking. While doing so he became aware of the behaviour the client was demonstrating. This will be discussed later in the chapter.

Eventually Patrick recognized that there was a high degree of consistency between his words and behaviour. (It was unfortunate that his client did not have the same level of insight.) Often classification of phenomena helps our understanding, so we now provide you with a classification of body language.

CLASSIFICATION OF BODY **LANGUAGE**

■ Emblems are those things that we do instead of, or for the purpose of reinforcing, a word, for example thumbs up, or thumb and forefinger making a circle thus saying everything is OK.

■ Illustrators are used to reinforce speech, for example, palm upright as if signalling stop or disagreement.

■ Regulators control interaction, and include things like verbal prompts or head movements.

■ Adapters are personal habits that we have developed, for example stroking the chin when talking. We probably are not aware of such idiosyncrasies. Finally our face is a very expressive organ, hence it is capable of showing many different kinds of emotion: fear, pleasure, boredom, confusion etc.

It is possible to break body language down into many component parts such as eye movements, sitting positions and facial expressions but one of the aspects which is often overlooked is the importance of hand gestures. In terms of honesty and deceit, open palms of the hand, that is facing the hands upwards, is a sign normally associated with honesty. The most obvious sign of this is where the person overtly and consciously raises his or her hands upward in order to say 'I am being honest' or 'I am telling you all I know.' Frequently the same sort of gesture is seen in a modified form, often as subtle as turning the hands upwards on the desk or table during a meeting.

Conversely, if people are attempting to deceive, they may turn their hands downwards or even seek to hide their hands beneath the table or behind their backs. If you are making a proposal and the person you are trying to influence is explaining why he or she cannot accept the recommendation and you notice these hand gestures, it could be that he or she is giving some invalid reason or excuse rather than a genuine objection. When used in the context of trying to deceive, the downward-facing hand gesture is often also linked to mannerisms such as avoiding eye contact and hand-to-face gestures.

In children the gestures tend to be more exaggerated; so a child who is lying may very obviously avoid looking the parent in the eye and may literally cover his or her mouth. In adult behaviour similar gestures are often seen but in a less obvious way. Examples of gestures which, when grouped with other non-verbal behaviours, may denote deception or lack of certainty about what is being said are covering the mouth with one hand or a few fingers, touching the nose or rubbing the eye, neck or ear.

It is important to be careful in the interpretation of non-verbal behaviour. Not only should one seek supporting evidence of the interpretation by looking for clusters which back up the initial assessment, but one should be aware of the significance of cultural differences. In some cultures, for instance, looking away and averting the gaze from the other person is considered disrespectful and could be interpreted as meaning lack of honesty, whereas in other cultures the opposite is true and it is considered respectful to look down and away from the other person.

SHOWING ASSUREDNESS

Just as there are certain clusters of behaviour that suggest uncertainty or deceit, so there are behaviours that suggest control and assertiveness. There is sometimes a thin line between signals that suggest confidence and those that might be interpreted as suggesting aggression. Consider, for instance, the difference between asking someone to do something with your hand held out with palms up (open gesture) and with your hand facing downwards (suggesting a directive approach) or even with one finger pointing (often interpreted as aggressive).

There are a number of significant hand gestures that provide valuable information about other people's frames of mind. If their hands are clenched, this often suggests some degree of frustration or that they are feeling negative and trying to resist direct confrontation. If you are attempting to influence by using a 'pull' approach and you detect holding back signals, it is worth considering whether you need to invest more time in understanding the other person's perspective; this would suggest the need for further listening skills and demonstration of empathy.

The pushing of the fingers of both hands together in an upward direction in order to create a 'steeple' is often associated with a person who is giving off signals of being or feeling in control or in a superior position. It may be that in your attempt to influence you wish to adopt a superior stance and would use such a gesture; however, if you are attempting to operate on a 'level playing field' then this will give entirely the wrong message.

Again a word of caution, because this sort of action is also sometimes associated with a quite different meaning, that of evaluation or consideration. In attempting to interpret the body language of the person you are trying to influence, the trick is to look for other evidence to support your initial assumption. So if you suspect a superior attitude and you see steepled hand gestures, the head raised upward, downward glances and a supercilious tone of voice, then you have reliable data on which to make your assessment of a dominant attitude. If, however, the steepled hand gestures are demonstrated at the same time as a pensive frown and thinking sounds such as 'Mm mm' then you are more likely to be faced with someone who is considering your idea or proposal.

In order to demonstrate confidence in a situation, as a general rule it is necessary to give strong assertive non-verbal messages without seeming aggressive. Achieving the right balance can be quite difficult; we list some examples of aggressive, passive and assertive non-verbal behaviours in Table 7.1.

MIRRORING AND **PACING**

One very practical application of non-verbal communication awareness is the use of mirroring and pacing techniques. Mirroring is, as the name

Table 7.1 Non-verbal behaviours

Aggressive	Passive	Assertive
	Avoiding the handshake	Initiating the handshake
Squeezing the other person's hand in a 'vice-like' grip	Offering a hand like a 'wet lettuce leaf' ie limp and floppy	Matching the other person with a strong and confident hand shake
Staring at the other person for protracted periods	Normally averting eye contact, only making the occasional sideways glance	Regularly making eye contact but focusing more on the forehead or bridge of the nose rather than staring directly into the eyes
Looming over the other person and invading his or her personal space	Shrinking back in the chair or if standing making oneself seem smaller	Sitting or standing upright
	Hands facing upwards and moving the body downwards	Hands facing downwards
Finger pointing and wagging at the other person	Touching one's own hand, arm, cuff or rings	Forearms on the desk or table, hands generally still unless using them to give support to a comment
Arms crossed and fists clenched		

implies, the process of copying the body language of the other person. This may sound rather ape-like behaviour and, if taken to extremes, this indeed is how it might be interpreted, and in this sense it could seem irritating. However, there is no doubt that when two or more people are engaged in a discussion, and they are getting on well together, they will start adopting similar sitting or standing positions and they will use similar gestures and mannerisms and even use the same terminology or verbal expressions.

Successful influencers will intuitively pick up on these points and will start to replay them to the person they are attempting to influence. It is possible to practise the skill of mirroring the other person in order to demonstrate that a strong rapport exists. This is really about taking your cues from the other person. Such mirroring behaviours could include:

■ sitting down when he or she sits down;
■ getting your papers or notes out at the same time;
■ engaging in small talk if he or she gives the signal;
■ standing, sitting or leaning in the same way;
■ using similar gestures;
■ using some of the same verbal expressions or terms;
■ using a similar tone or speaking at the same level.

In a similar way it is possible to identify the pace at which the other person is operating and to adopt a similar pace in the discussion. In order to influence effectively it is necessary to be sensitive to such matters and, in the initial stage at least, to operate at a similar pace. There is nothing to be gained from racing ahead with your point of view if the other person is not mentally ready.

In the same way, if you pick up signs that the other person wishes to move the discussion on at some pace, then it is important to recognize this and to respond accordingly, rather than pursuing a protracted line in small talk. Having recognized and matched the other person's pace, it may then be possible to lead the pace, in other words, to increase the pace of the discussion, or slow it down, to suit your needs.

Proponents of NLP would suggest that it is possible to mirror and pace right down to the level of the other person's thinking and breathing patterns, though here we are concerned with some of the more obvious and clear-cut patterns of non-verbal behaviour.

PAUSE FOR **THOUGHT**

1. *What signs do you show when you are being defensive?*
2. *Consider and list the types of positive body language you use when you are influencing somebody.*

3. *When you are next attempting to influence someone consider the following:*

■ *How often do you change position?*
■ *Are any of your gestures similar to his or hers?*
■ *Can you detect the pace at which he or she wants to move through the discussion?*

Try matching non-verbal behaviour without mimicking every move. Also look out for whether he or she starts mirroring your non-verbal behaviour. Consider how you feel this affects the process of communication.

IMPACT OF CULTURAL DIFFERENCES ON BODY **LANGUAGE**

Earlier in the chapter we referred to the importance of recognizing that there may be significant cultural differences as to how people communicate non-verbally and the interpretation of specific approaches.

A useful distinction has been made by Trompenaars (1993) between what he refers to as 'neutral' and 'affective' cultures. In neutral cultures, often associated with the UK, the East Coast of the United States, Japan and Scandinavia, the tendency is towards neutral non-verbal behaviour. The emphasis is on self-control, and overt displays of feelings tend to be frowned upon. In these cultures, hand movements tend to be more restricted and tone of voice is more even throughout the discussion. There is likely to be an unwritten code of conduct as to who speaks when, and interruptions are likely to be quite discreet. If a person feels angry or upset, this is less likely to be shown through frequent displays of emotion. It is not to say that emotion is never shown, but that it is more likely to be held inside the individual for as long as possible. The consequence of this is that emotion may then be displayed in the occasional cathartic dumping or even channelled toward people or activities other than those causing it.

By contrast, in affective cultures, more often associated with Latin, Arabic and South American countries and the West Coast of the United States, there is much more animation in the process of communication, and emotions are more likely to be displayed overtly, even to relative strangers. So in an affective culture people are likely to rely heavily on body language such as facial expression and hand and arm gestures in order to support the verbal messages being conveyed. Tone of voice will tend to have a wide range of modulation and it is considered quite acceptable to interrupt and talk over the other person without him or her taking offence. It is not unusual to see a high level of physical contact in communication. Back-slapping, patting, touching and hugging, which might seem rather over-demonstrative in a neutral culture, are all a normal part of communication in an affective culture.

So if these are accepted as cultural norms, then what are the implications of this for the influencing situation? Simply being aware of the differences is an important starting point. It is unrealistic to believe that, if you are working in a culture different from your own, you will be able to change the way others operate in order to fit in with your cultural norm. What is more likely is that you will need to be sensitive to the differences and make allowances. So an Italian working in the UK may naturally feel the people are more frosty or formal in their style of communication, but conversely a British subject working in Italy could find discussions too unruly and emotional. Similarly a Californian working in Japan could feel frustrated at the lack of non-verbal feedback to a presentation. The key is to question whether the behaviour stems from broad cultural differences rather than being a reaction to an individual. While it is difficult to change one's own behaviour radically, and indeed there is an argument that we should celebrate our cultural diversity, it can be helpful to modify one's behaviour in the direction of the other person.

An interesting question to consider is whether organizations, as well as nations, have neutral or affective cultures. Certainly some organizations are much more ordered, clinical and unemotional in their style whereas others encourage emotion and expression of feelings. Again it is worth considering the norms for your own organization and for those in which you do business because radical differences could be presenting significant barriers to the process of influencing.

We have looked at the importance of body language and how it can impact on influencing. As indicated at the start of the chapter, body language plays a critical role in all interactive stages of the Model of Successful Influencing. In order to influence others successfully, it is important to be aware of the signals that we give others as well as being able to read and interpret the body language of others. The secret is to look for clusters or groups of behaviour rather than pinning all the meaning on just one characteristic.

We now turn our attention to the issue of handling put-offs. As with body language, the need to recognize and deal with put-offs is an aspect of influencing that is not confined to one stage of the influencing process. Put-offs can and will occur at any stage, which explains the central position of put-offs in the diagrammatic representation of the Model of Successful Influencing.

eight

DEALING WITH PUT-OFFS

In this chapter we:

- explore the notion of assertiveness primarily as a philosophy of personal responsibility;
- explore a continuum of behaviour ranging from passive or submissive, through assertive, to aggressive, and examine the consequences of each;
- explain the steps, and examine the basic techniques, of assertion;
- consider ways of confronting other people and demonstrate how to say 'no' effectively;
- consider the stages through which relationships pass when they are in decline, while at the same time exploring strategies for managing differences;
- explore the subject of human emotion, in particular how we can control our own anger and manage situations where others become angry.

So far in the Model of Successful Influencing we have looked at all the stages, starting with planning, then moving through pleasantries, preface, position and problems, and following on to possibilities, preferences and positive action. We explored the subject of body language in influencing. In this chapter we will consider the subject of how to manage the confrontational situations which may occur at any stage of the influencing process.

Successful influencers whom we interviewed as part of our research consistently showed the ability to confront others in an assertive way and to remain calm, displaying controlled demeanour, often when those around them strained under pressure. When we examined their behaviour under pressure we discovered that there were some specific techniques which can be taught (and learnt).

Our practical international experience with thousands of different individuals through the design and delivery of 'The Power of Personal Influence Programme' has shown us that practising the skills and techniques of assertion can in fact result in significant behavioural change. Such change can be accelerated if combined with mental practice and the use of cognitive techniques such as self-assertion statements.

To begin with we will discuss a range of behaviours positioned on what we will refer to as 'the assertiveness continuum'.

THE ASSERTIVENESS **CONTINUUM**

What do you think of when you hear the term 'assertiveness'? When we ask this question to groups of managers we often hear comments such as:

- 'getting your own way';
- 'being able to say what you think';
- 'standing up for your rights';
- 'staying cool under pressure';
- 'the ability to deal with difficult situations'.

All of these definitions are, in part, correct. They refer to the subject of assertiveness, however, primarily from the point of view of the person being assertive. We consider assertiveness to be a philosophy; a way of thinking about oneself and about others that is manifested though our behaviour as well as in the use of specific verbal techniques.

The assertive philosophy is about believing in the value of the individual (oneself) and by definition the value of other people. Assertiveness means respecting the rights of both parties in an influencing situation. It is not about getting your own way every time, nor is it simply a series of techniques providing a way to manipulate others while appearing to be considerate. Simply put, assertiveness is about **saying the right things, in the right way, at the right time.**

Clearly it is easier to achieve one or two out of three in this definition; getting three out of three is significantly more difficult. This is compounded by the fact that the times when we most need to remain assertive are those when there is a danger of emotion, in particular the emotion of anger, either our own or that of others, overtaking us. For example there are many situations where a person does or says something which we may find annoying or with which we strongly disagree, and we have to decide whether to confront him or her, or not. We have nearly all thought at some time after such an event, 'I wish I had told her. . .' or 'I should have said. . .', but do we actually confront the person? There may be other situations where you do attempt to confront him or her, but either you find that your message becomes confused and weakened or the whole thing escalates and becomes confused by emotional displays such as anger.

It is interesting, though, to note that everyone has a tendency to react in difficult situations with particular behaviour from the range constituting the assertiveness continuum. Figure 8.1 shows the assertiveness continuum as a line of behaviours with aggressive behaviour at one end and passive behaviour at the other. The midpoint shows the types of behaviour we describe as assertive, and it is in fact the competence of assertion that we believe to be the most appropriate in the majority of influencing situations.

'Assertion' is the word that describes a range of skills that will tend to result in the following benefits:

- being honest with yourself and others;
- saying what you want, need, think and feel (but not at the expense of others);
- confidence and positive behaviour, and being prepared to move towards a workable compromise which respects the rights and needs of both parties.

Before we try to understand the concept of assertiveness, first let us look in more detail at the behaviours at both ends of the continuum. In order to illustrate the range of behaviours, we will describe the extreme examples. It should be recognized that very few people operate at the extremes all the time and those that do will tend to suffer from social and possibly even serious psychological problems. When we have described the passive and aggressive extremes and the assertive ideal, we will ask you to consider where you think you sit on the continuum in terms of your normal style for dealing with difficult situations.

Passive	Assertive	Aggressive
I lose	I win	I win
You win	You win	You lose

Figure 8.1 The assertiveness continuum

AGGRESSIVE BEHAVIOUR

Aggressive behaviour can best be described as an approach which works on the basis that 'I win and you lose'; the rights of the other person are not necessarily recognized and it is assumed that the way to achieve things is to take from others and force them into submission. People who operate at this extreme of the continuum tend to have learnt their predominant behaviours from a very early age. So the child who learned to get what he wanted by taking from other children would, if successful, have learnt that such aggressive approaches work. This would be likely to have led him to use such approaches throughout later life.

In extremes cases aggressive behaviour is seen in organizations where adult bullies achieve things through the use of force, threats, harassment, coercion, fear and the intimidation of others. Such people tend to be extremely competitive, to the extent that they will always want to play win–lose games. They will be prepared to do this not only against the competition but also against other departments, or even colleagues. They do not mind if this is at the expense of their relationships with others.

A range of verbal and non-verbal behaviours can identify aggressive people. They are likely to be preoccupied with themselves and will tend to use a telling style in managing others. They will give feedback to others in a judgmental way, and are less likely to give constructive advice about how things could be improved. They will use sarcasm and cutting one-line comments to put people down, for example 'You would say that, wouldn't you?' or 'Yes, but that's only your view' or 'What do you know?' They will also use threats in order to force people to do things, so will tend to use phrases such as 'I'm warning you' or 'If you don't do this then. . .'.

The non-verbal behaviour of aggressive people might include frequent raising of the voice or even shouting, abrupt speech and extreme sharp hand gestures such as finger pointing and clenching of the fist. Facially, aggressive people will push their chin forward and they will tend to scowl and frown in a threatening or doubting way, particularly when listening to others presenting their case. They are likely to overemphasize staring at the other person and will seek to adopt a dominant sitting or standing position, frequently invading the personal space of the other person. Of course some people are very successful in using this style of behaviour and they may find themselves rising to senior positions in organizations. What do you think the consequences are of such behaviour?

Aggressive people tend ultimately to become socially isolated as those around them, either consciously or unconsciously, keep their distance or decide to combat the aggression with aggression. What is interesting about the response of some people when confronted with the overtly aggressive approach is that they may seem to accept this behaviour, but covertly they may seek to 'pay the other person back'. This concept of payback is an important one because it may be demonstrated in very subtle ways without the person on the receiving end knowing that it is happening. Consider the following story-board that is based on an actual meeting from a real organization.

Storyboard: Long-term payback

Sarah worked for a major public-transport organization and had recently been promoted from a corporate personnel role to a senior management position heading up one of the operating divisions.

She had been told when promoted that the division seemed to be very set in its ways and that part of her role was to encourage a more forward-thinking approach amongst the managers.

She had recognized right from the start of her new role that there was a considerable amount of underlying tension between the various middle managers for whom she was responsible. Interestingly she had detected this, not from obvious displays of tension but from the unnaturally high level of politeness.

In one of the management meetings she decided to turn the meeting over to an organizational development exercise, a potentially high-risk strategy that she hoped would confront some of the blockages. Her approach was to explain that, as part of the opening up of communications, she wanted each of the 10 managers in the room to think of the one thing he or she disliked most about the person sitting opposite. She then asked each to stand up and point at the person and tell him or her what was particularly disliked and why. She felt that by using this type of approach she was likely to get to the real issues of underlying tension.

It was the response of the first manager to speak that was most telling. He pointed across the room and said, 'I remember in 1967 when we were trainees, you lost some of your technical equipment and you borrowed my tool kit. Although you promised to return everything, I never did get it all back, despite asking several times.' This manager recounted the story as though it had just happened, despite the fact that he was remembering an action from many, many years before, when he was in his apprentice-ship.

The fascinating issue here is that the manager had not overtly confronted the aggressor before being pushed to do so through Sarah's unusual intervention. If he had borne a grudge all these years, the question this raises is, what had he done over this period to 'pay him back'?

Payback is the behaviour we see when someone feels that he or she has been dealt with in an aggressive manner. The key point about payback is that it can, as in the case described above, take place over a protracted period of time, and the nature of the payback is often disproportionate to the original issue.

So in the above example the manager who was aggrieved was likely, over a period of many years, to have paid back the aggressor several times over. And to make matters worse, the nature of the payback may well have been through the use of manipulative or covert means; in other words, the original aggressor may have been getting paid back without even knowing it. Such payback could have taken the form of, for instance:

- spreading rumours through the informal grapevine;
- adversely influencing his staff;
- creating situations where the other person could lose face and credibility publicly;
- failing to co-operate with requests for help;
- withholding critical information.

It should be noted that aggressive behaviour can be classified further as either aggressive manipulative, which is nearer to the centre or aggressive hostile, nearer to the extreme.

Often people who operate at the aggressive extreme end of the continuum tend to live their lives on the brink of abnormal behaviour. Their extreme competitive nature means they might compete with their own colleagues, staff, friends and even children. Insecurity and intense anxiety drive their behaviour; they tend to be driven by a need constantly to impose themselves and their views on others. The consequence of this is that they are prone to the effects of stress, the result of such extreme behaviours.

It may seem from the outside that such people are successful in the obvious sense of getting what they want, because the effects of such behaviour are not always obviously seen. Ultimately, however, extremely aggressive people are likely, if privately, to feel lonely, isolated and stressed. Increasingly they will question the validity of their own existences.

PASSIVE BEHAVIOUR

By contrast with aggressive behaviour, passive behaviour describes the 'I lose and you win' mind-set. People who operate at this extreme of the continuum always put the rights of others before their own rights, the assumption displayed being that other people are of more value. Examples of passive behaviour would be:

- agreeing to give time to an activity to which you are not really committed;
- allowing someone to say something about you that you feel is unjustified, but not challenging him or her;
- apologizing to others for taking up their time when you have something to say to them;
- saying 'yes' when you really want to say 'no';
- making up spurious or tangential excuses for not doing something rather than explaining the real reasons;
- taking the blame for something for which someone else is responsible;
- failing to intervene in a group discussion when a decision is being made about something with which you disagree.

It is not difficult to identify people who are at the passive extreme of the assertiveness continuum. They often fail to have their voices heard at meetings. If they dare to try to voice opinions, other stronger characters speak more loudly. Passive people give up easily. They are likely to think, 'Oh, he has a better point to make than me. I could never compete with him. Anyway, my views are not that important.'

Verbally, passive people may use roundabout ways of saying anything with which the other person could disagree. Their fear is of offending others, and of being drawn into any form of confrontation. As opposed to aggressive people who put other people down, passive people will overtly put themselves down with comments such as 'I don't know much about this but. . .' or 'I'm sorry for taking up your time on this' or, in a group discussion when it comes to their turn to speak, they will say, 'How could I possibly follow that – my question is going to seem really silly, but what I would like to say is. . .' as though to suggest that they are in no way as important as the other person.

Just as aggressive people will overtly evaluate other people negatively, passive people will negatively evaluate themselves; so they will say, 'I am no good at this' or 'I really need to improve my ability at. . .'.

In a similar way the non-verbal behaviour of passive people can be seen as the opposite of aggressive. They will back away and place themselves in submissive positions, often making themselves seem physically smaller. They will look away rather than making direct eye contact and their voices are likely to be hesitant, quiet and apologetic in tone. Clearly we are painting the picture of an extreme here, but such people do exist and, as with the aggressive style, the passive style is often learnt at a very early stage in life. So for young children, passive behaviour may be rewarded by others feeling sympathetic or sorry for them. They learn that the way to get what you want is to opt for the 'sympathy vote', to act helpless and hope that others will seek to save them. And yes, some people will save them and feel sorry for them – up to a point. Eventually the sympathy may turn to pity and loss of respect. It is also worth noting that passive behaviour stems from insecurity and anxiety, and leaves the person vulnerable to the predatory behaviour of aggressive individuals. So others, particularly those at the aggressive end of the continuum, will take advantage of their passive behaviour in order to make sure the passive person does indeed 'lose'.

The consequence of this is that the self-esteem of passive people will be particularly low. When asked how they feel about their lives, they will say they feel used. This should not be a surprise because those who are happy to take advantage of them do use them. Over long periods of time this can lead to intense frustration, low self-esteem and even ill health.

The real danger is that such passive behaviour will lead to a build-up of emotion and anger, which is kept hidden from others. Suppressed anger slowly builds into resentment until such time as there is a spontaneous explosion; and then it is not uncommon to witness what we describe as 'anger transference'. This is where the person is no longer able to control his or her feelings and there is a cathartic dumping of emotions onto one person in one situation. The target is usually an easy one, and often different from the source of the anger; for that reason some psychologists will refer to this concept as 'displacement', as the anger or frustration is displaced to an innocent party. For example the manager who, over time, feels a build-up of pressure as result of being put upon in a work situation, may transfer his or her anger onto family; or the business traveller who has put up with a difficult journey to the other side of the world, having missed trains and been delayed at airports, may on arrival at the destination hotel find that a room has not been booked. This might result in a dramatic explosion of emotion and anger all directed at the receptionist, and totally disproportionate to the given situation.

The skill of the receptionist in this case is to remain calm under pressure, and we will look at this competence of controlled demeanour later in the chapter. Often the consequence of anger transference is that the individual feels guilty, particularly as the anger subsides and he or she returns to a more natural style. As a result of this guilt or discomfort, he or she may engage in various psychological defence mechanisms like rationalization or atoning.

Having discussed the two extremes of the assertiveness continuum, we will now look in detail at the competence of assertion which, in most influencing situations, is the preferred option.

ASSERTIVE BEHAVIOUR

In many situations where there is a conflict of interests it is all too easy to be drawn into an emotional and hostile confrontation. Assertive behaviour is about seeking win–win solutions where there is an outcome which both parties accept and believe in, even though both people may approach the situation from different perspectives.

With an assertive approach, however, it is possible to accept and understand the differences without allowing them to destroy the relationship. This calls for a measure of self-control and discipline, and we will look at some of the psychological aspects of how it is possible to control one's emotions. Our experience of teaching the skills of assertion has shown that it is possible to learn the steps of assertion and also its techniques. By learning and practising them in real situations, and combining this with the appropriate metacognition, it is possible to bring about real and lasting changes in the ability to be assertive.

Let us now consider the recommended pattern or steps of assertion when providing an assertive response to another person.

The steps of assertion

The first step is to show others that we are listening and that we understand their point of view. This does not mean that we necessarily agree with what they have said, but importantly it recognizes their right to say what they think, and acknowledges their need, albeit a different one from ours.

This step requires the skills of active listening, which we discussed in Chapter 5. Listening is not enough, but we have to show we are listening. It is a particularly important step in assertion for those whose natural tendency would be to operate at the more aggressive end of the assertiveness continuum; it is important for such people to resist the temptation to jump in with their own views straight away. When the other person is presenting an argument or point of view, with which you happen to disagree, maintaining a controlled approach to active listening is admittedly difficult. The danger is that one resorts to a push approach (pushing your own views) rather than a pull approach (identifying the views of others and working with rather than against their arguments) to influencing.

Only once you have genuinely understood the other person's viewpoint should you move on to the second step of assertiveness. At this point, you should say what you think, need, feel and want. You will not necessarily get it, but it should be seen as your desired outcome. It may be that through the use of strong active listening skills you find out that your perspective is not as different from the other person's as you initially assumed. If so, then having discovered this at an early stage of the interaction can prevent a polarization of perspectives early on, and thus reduce the likelihood of becoming involved in the 'locking of horns' that is commonly associated with conflict situations.

People who are generally at the aggressive end of the continuum do not usually have difficulty with this step. However, saying what you want and feel is especially important, and potentially more difficult, for those people who are more passive.

Third, having explained what you think and feel, it is then necessary to say what you want to happen. It is unlikely that you will get this, but it is this third step that forms a basis from which you can seek a workable compromise.

Workable compromise is the key; it means seeking a solution which will satisfy the needs of both parties; it implies that both sides will need to give a little if a win–win is to be achieved. It may be possible for each party to concede something and to gain something else or, even better, it may be possible to find a solution that neither person had previously considered and which results in a gain for everyone concerned. In the absence of such an outcome, one party will perceive him or herself as winner and the others will see themselves as losers, with all the resultant consequences.

So in summary the steps of assertion are:

1. Show listening and understanding.
2. Say what you think, feel, need or want.
3. Say what you want to happen.
4. Search for a workable compromise.

To illustrate how the steps of assertion can work in practice we will take a real work-based example.

Storyboard: The steps of assertion

Paul is team leader of a software engineering team in a high-technology engineering organization, and one of his responsibilities is to manage the contract software engineers working in his area.

An inherent difficulty in this working relationship is that the contract staff have little real loyalty to the organization; they are on short fixed-term contracts, earning high rates of pay, and then they move on to other organizations. In addition, they are leading-edge experts in their subject and have invaluable expertise that is vital to the success of the project.

Naturally this makes management of the contract engineers more problematic; it is not possible for Paul to rely purely on position power. He has to use his personal influencing skills in order to obtain their co-operation.

Consider the following exchange where Paul uses the steps of assertion in order to manage what might have been a difficult situation. You will notice from the comments against some of his statements that he also uses techniques of assertion that we discuss in more detail later in the chapter.

It is Thursday afternoon, the project is under extreme pressure to deliver against a tight time-scale and Paul has to organize the schedule of staffing for the weekend. Jayne is one of the contract engineers in the project team.

JAYNE: Paul, I was wondering if I could take the day off tomorrow; something has come up which I need to deal with at home.

PAUL: Ah, Jayne, I was just working on the scheduling for the next two weeks, and I needed to sort out the shifts for the team. Tell me, what exactly is it that you are looking for?

(**active listening**)

JAYNE: Well, I just need tomorrow off so I can sort out a few things.

PAUL: I see. . .mm mm. . .

(**active listening**: using pauses, silence and non-verbal prompts.)

JAYNE: Well, if you must know, I'm having a few problems with my partner, and we've agreed to take some time off to really sort ourselves out.

PAUL: Oh, I see, Jayne. I'm sorry to hear that you're having a difficult time. I know it can be quite stressful, particularly when you've a busy job. I'm sure you know best how to deal with the situation, but if there's anything I can do to help I would be only too pleased.

(**active listening**: showing empathy.)

JAYNE: That's very kind of you, Paul. The main thing I need is time, to be honest. Can I assume it would be OK to take tomorrow off?

(**broken record technique**: Jayne is using the broken record technique to assert her needs; we discuss this technique later on.)

PAUL: No, that'll not be possible, Jayne. However, I do believe we can come to an arrangement that's good for both of us. I feel there's a need to draw on all the team at this stage of the project. In fact, to be frank, I'm under quite some pressure myself, Jayne.

(**state what you feel**: Paul is making it clear how he feels about the situation. He has also taken an effective approach to saying no, which is to say the actual word 'no' and to say it upfront and early in the discussion. He uses the word 'however', being careful not to fuel the confrontation with emotionally provocative language. He uses the technique of self-disclosure in revealing his own circumstances, which can help in building the strength of the relationship.)

JAYNE: So you're saying I can't take time off to deal with the problem, Paul?

PAUL: No, I'm not saying that, Jayne. What I am saying is that I want to have the whole team on site tomorrow. It may be possible to make a few hours of time available if we can find some way of getting cover for you. Is there any possibility that you could come in tomorrow for half a day?

JAYNE: Well, I suppose I could, but I really must have the discussion tomorrow before the weekend because we're not together from Saturday on for a week and things are really coming to a head. Would it be possible for me to come in really early and then to leave by 10 o'clock?

PAUL: I'm sure that would be OK if you could find someone from another team who is looking for some overtime who might be able to cover for you.

(**workable compromise**: Paul is clearly seeking a workable compromise. He is looking to meet Jayne's needs without weakening his own position on staffing cover for the weekend. He also places some responsibility on Jayne to help resolve the problem.)

JAYNE: Well, I suppose that's only fair, Paul. As a matter of fact, I know that Systems Group have some people who feel a little under-utilized — maybe I'll have a word with Kurt.

In the example above, Paul follows the steps of assertion by showing Jayne that he is listening and understands her point of view before stating how he feels, what he wants and working towards a compromise which satisfies the needs of both himself and Jayne.

The true test of assertion is whether the dignity and esteem of both parties are left intact at the end of the day. Paul might have taken an aggressive approach by insisting that Jayne should work when he required it, without taking any notice of her views or feelings. Equally if he had taken a passive approach and simply accepted Jayne's demand for time off without questioning it, she might have taken advantage of it, and his role in managing the project would have been undermined.

We identified in the storyboard that, as well as working through the steps of assertion, Paul used certain techniques of assertion. We will now look in more detail at a range of techniques that can be deployed, particularly in confrontational situations where you hold different views from the person you are attempting to influence.

THE TECHNIQUES OF **ASSERTION**

We now identify nine techniques of assertion, which we discuss in the section below. One concern some people raise when discussing these techniques is that it may be possible to define them in theory, but in practice it is difficult to remember them all and they can seem rehearsed or artificial when used.

Well, in part we would agree with this argument; it is more difficult to use such techniques in the early stages of learning them. However, by learning and practising them in a systematic way and persevering over time, managers can be seen significantly to increase their repertoire of skills when faced with confrontational situations.

Incidentally, we have just used one of the most powerful techniques of assertion, which we refer to as 'fogging'. This is where, when faced with an argument with which you disagree, you start by agreeing with the other person's point of view, but only in part. You then present your counter-argument. The trick with fogging is to deflate the impact of the other person's argument by agreeing with him or her just when you are expected to disagree. This has the effect of 'fogging' or limiting the hostility of the interaction; by coming in at a later stage with your own views, you show that you are not necessarily diametrically opposed in your respective positions, but that you have some areas of agreement and some issues to resolve.

When people are angry they do things that attract attention to themselves, for example, raising their voices or banging the table. The use of fogging lowers the temperature by recognizing and legitimizing the angry person's need to be noticed. Once he or she has had the signal 'It's OK to be angry', the anger starts to dissipate.

From a personal perspective it is important, when facing confrontational situations, to control one's inner dialogues. We discussed the concept of inner dialogues in some detail in Chapters 3 and 4. In confrontational situations it is important first of all to recognize the nature of our inner dialogues. Typically in confrontational situations, inner dialogues tend to be negative. So in the storyboard example, it would not be unusual for Paul, on realizing the nature of Jayne's request, to follow a line of inner dialogue such as:

> Oh, here we go again. The staff are always trying to find reasons for not pulling their weight. This project's turning out to be a nightmare in terms of administration. Jayne is using the sympathy line again – it's strange how everyone has a major personal problem when it comes to working hard. And what is more these contractors, they really do try it on – they know they can hold us to ransom. I know if I don't give her time off she'll resent it. It'll only reflect in her work. And what's more, she'll tell other people that I'm a tyrant. I can't seem to win in this job – I've got the customers shouting at me for delivery and the senior management pressing me to control the budget, and the staff who are uncontrollable.

Notice how in this example of an inner dialogue Paul gradually convinces himself that he is in a situation he is unable to control; this belief in itself is likely to be the cause of significant personal stress. The dialogue is largely inaccurate, and Paul would be better advised to engage in positive inner dialogues. So he might say: 'Jayne must be having a difficult time at the moment. I would like to help her, but I must keep momentum going. Generally, I have a lot of committed and talented staff. I'm sure between us we can pull the project through what's proving to be a challenging time.'

One of the key techniques in dealing with conflict is to be aware of our inner dialogues, and to check whether they are rational. Another important point is to recognize that we can control inner dialogues before, during and after difficult events.

As to the external verbal dialogue, it is important to respond, and not simply to react on an emotional basis. The danger with reacting emotionally, rather than responding to the information provided by the other person, is that we tend to make assumptions about his or her position and views. Misplaced inner dialogues often fuel these assumptions and serve to polarize positions. In practice this may require us to count to 10 or 100 or 1,000, whatever it takes to give us time to give a measured response rather than a knee-jerk reflex action.

We mentioned in the storyboard that Paul was selective in his use of language: he used the word 'however', which is much less confrontational than 'but'. Taking care with language is often a matter of subtlety: consider, for instance, the different impact of the following two statements, which are intended to convey the same message: 'I have called this meeting to discuss the problem I have with you' and 'There are a few issues I feel we could usefully discuss.' The first example could be construed as quite personal and threatening, whereas the second example suggests more of a joint problem-solving approach. The key point with the use of language in potentially confrontational situations is to think about how the words you select could be construed by the other person; often words and comments which seem quite innocuous to us can be interpreted by others in a very different way.

It is also important when confronting others to check our body language. There is a danger that facial expressions, gestures, our sitting position or stance and tone of voice will be interpreted in ways that we did not intend. This becomes a hindrance if it polarizes positions, and the skill is to be aware of the messages we are giving out through our body language and to check that they are consistent with our verbal communication. If verbal and non-verbal communications are in conflict, then the other person is intuitively likely to read along the non-verbal channel for the real meaning. It is no good strictly adhering to the steps of assertion if we get so close as to threaten the other person or, alternatively, if we draw back and make ourselves insignificant.

Ken and Kate Back, in their book *Assertiveness at Work* (1982), identify a number of different types of assertion, some of which are particularly relevant to the influencing situation. They use the term 'discrepancy assertion' to describe the assertive technique whereby we point out the differences between what a person is saying and what he or she is doing; so in the storyboard example, Paul might use discrepancy assertion and say: 'Jayne, you said that you would be prioritizing more time on project A; however, I've noticed that you're still spending all your time on project B. I wonder how you feel about this?'

Discrepancy assertion also deals with the difference between two discrepant messages received from the same person. So again in the storyboard example, Paul might say: 'Jayne, I'm a little uncertain as to what you're saying here. First of all you said the problem was a domestic one and then you mentioned that it was really to do with your frustration with the job: could you clarify which is the real issue here?'

Discrepancy assertion is a particularly useful technique to use when the other person is becoming emotional; when in an emotional state, it is likely that he or she will hurl lots of different problems at you, some of them genuine and some spurious. Discrepancy assertion helps you distinguish between the emotional and the real issues.

Negative feelings assertion is another technique, one which is particularly useful when you feel yourself becoming emotional. It is where you point out to the other person the effect his or her behaviour is having on you. So if Jayne is becoming hostile to Paul, and he is finding it difficult to control the discussion, he might use negative feelings assertion in the following way: 'Jayne, I have to say that when you thump the desk and raise your voice in this way, it makes it very difficult for me to concentrate. I don't feel this is helping our discussion. I understand that you may be very angry, and I can understand why; however, just standing there and shouting at me doesn't help us to move things forward.'

Negative feelings assertion is a way of, in a figurative sense, holding a mirror up to the other person to show how he or she is behaving and to let him or her know the effect it is having on you or on others. In the above example of negative feelings assertion, Paul states what he feels while also showing some empathy for the way Jayne may feel. The use of negative feelings assertion is also a way of expressing your feelings without being drawn into an emotional situation.

The broken record technique is a simple but effective way of asserting your views to the other person and is the approach of repeating, like a broken record, the key point that you want the other to hear and understand. This is the approach taken by the young child who uses the broken record technique to persuade his or her parents to buy an ice-cream; by the fourth or fifth time of asking, having previously had the request declined, the child has worn the parents down, and they concede. Often the same sort of approach can be used, but in a more subtle way, through saying the same thing in a slightly different way.

Finally, we believe a powerful technique of assertion and one to be used only as a last resort when other techniques do not seem to be working, is the ABC technique for giving powerful feedback to others. It works in the following way:

Action	We describe the situation or context of the other person's actions
Behaviour	We go on to describe the behaviour we observe
Consequence	Finally, we explain the consequences of such behaviour, in other words the action we or others may take if the behaviour does not change

So in the storyboard example, if Jayne were failing to gain any co-operation from Paul despite several attempts to seek time off, she might use the ABC technique by saying: 'We have been discussing the matter of time off for some time now' (**action**) 'and you have on four separate occasions blocked my requests without making any alternative suggestions' (**behaviour**). 'If you continue to block all my attempts to find a way around the problem, then I will have no choice but to ask the human resource department to transfer me to another project' (**consequence**).

The key issue with the ABC technique is that this is not about making threats to try to coerce the other person into doing what you want them to do. It is about simply stating in a factual way what the consequences will be if the other person fails to change his or her behaviour, and it should be used as a last resort.

SAYING NO **EFFECTIVELY**

Another key issue, which is frequently the cause of a great deal of stress, is the inability to say no to others. Saying no in the right way is important when influencing; not saying no may lead to unwanted outcomes. This is particularly an issue for those who are more passive, who are likely to feel very guilty about saying no to others for fear of offending. Such people will often go to great trouble to say anything other than no when responding to requests. They will, in extreme cases, agree to do things and accept comments from others with which they do not really agree.

We have found when studying the behaviour of successful influencers that they tend to be capable of saying no without feeling guilty and without fuelling a confrontation. The way they say no, however, tends to follow a certain pattern. It is effective in that others accept the no for what it is rather than attempting to come back repeatedly with the same request, with the resultant feelings of guilt. We summarize the rules for saying no as follows:

1. **Say no and say it early**
   This means you should say the actual word 'no' rather than, as is often the case, using any other word than no. Frequently people will use words or expressions such as 'maybe', 'possibly', 'I am not sure' or 'Could I get back to you on that?' rather than actually saying no. The danger here is that the other person will interpret such responses as meaning that there is an opportunity to come back and make the request again hoping for a yes. Because we tend to listen intently to the first things others say, special care needs to be taken to ensure that the actual word 'no' is said early in your response, rather than tagging it on almost as an after-thought.

2. **Take care with apologies**
   When declining a request from another person, it is necessary to be careful not to over-apologize. If you do so it weakens the strength of your argument and implies that you should be saying yes. It also sends out a signal to the other person that if he or she were to come back to you with the request, you might eventually say yes.

3. **Avoid excessive elaboration**
    In a similar way it is difficult for others to accept your point of view if you spend too much time elaborating on the reasons why you are unable to do something. This may be seen as excuse-making and is also often interpreted as meaning that you could be persuaded if the person were to persist.

4. **Offer an alternative**
    It is helpful if, rather than just saying no, you are able to offer some options with which both parties can be satisfied. This is about seeking workable compromise, and it may be possible to identify how you could meet the other person halfway or to identify a solution that he or she had not considered. Of all the possibilities, this appeared to be the most significant in terms of making the other person feel OK about the refusal.

When dealing with put-offs, we run the risk of damaging relationships. You will remember the model of the stages relationships pass through on the way to maturity. We now consider the issue of relationships in decline.

RELATIONSHIPS IN **DECLINE**

When a relationship begins to fail the first stage is **differentiating**. This early stage of relationship breakdown starts to show when parties make their differences public, with greater emphasis on individualism. Communication tends to move from being joint towards being unilateral. The individuals focus on each other and at this level a great deal of the behaviour will be face-saving. They are judgmental of each other, which leads to the next stage, **stagnation**.

At this point communication between the parties diminishes and, when together, there is an avoidance of sensitive areas. Issues will fail to be resolved, which might well lead to feelings of frustration. There is a considerable degree of mistrust and ultimately things move into the next stage of **avoidance**. By now the parties have minimal contact with each other and when communication does take place it may well be systematized or formal. Personal attacks will be common, with behaviours tending toward revenge rather than conflict resolution. The final stage is one of **termination** in which one or both parties, formally or informally, terminate the relationship.

Recognition that the relationship is breaking down is the first step towards seeking a successful resolution. In severe cases, outside assistance may be necessary. Once decline has been recognized, the downward cycle can be broken. How?

Agree the ground rules for communication:

1. Receive the other person's comments without interruption or allowing yourself to become defensive.
2. Summarize the other person's comments.
3. Request that the other person proposes a way forward or suggests a way the problem can be resolved.
4. Review and discuss options before agreeing the way forward.

PAUSE FOR **THOUGHT**

1. *Consider a difficult working relationship. What stage are you at now using the model we have described?*
2. *Could you turn this decline around?*
3. *What are you planning to do about this decline?*

As you will recognize, relationships go through phases. It will be difficult if not impossible to influence a person if our relationship is in decline. We will always encounter some individuals with whom it is more difficult for us to form productive relationships. When facing hostility from others, our psychology is such that we are likely naturally to adopt a 'fight' or 'flight' response; in other words, either we will feel the urge to stand up for our rights and fight in order to protect ourselves, or we will make an instinctive decision that the best route to self-preservation is to escape and avoid the fight. These instincts date back to our prehistoric roots. Our behaviour has been modified considerably as we have developed; however, it is still possible to observe behaviours that have their roots in the fight and flight response.

A critical skill in influencing is the ability to manage one's own emotions and keep control; this means sticking to facts and responding to others rather than reacting. Some people are in jobs where there is a particular need for controlled demeanour because they are in the firing line for attacks from the customer; think, for instance, of the hotel receptionist or the airport desk attendant. In this sort of role, employees are taught how to deal with complaints in such a way that emotion becomes diffused and the relationship with the customer is maintained. It is quite a skill because it often means not only taking control of one's own emotions but also managing the emotions of the other person. While it may not be possible to control the emotions of others, it is possible to use a number of techniques to help them control their own.

The successful influencers who took part in our research displayed strong ability to remain calm when those around them were becoming flustered and emotional; furthermore, they also showed an ability to have a calming and placating effect when others became emotional.

INTERNAL CONTROL

The ability to maintain a controlled demeanour begins with recognizing the emotion we are starting to experience, and this means being aware of the physiological changes taking place, which indicate that such emotions are coming to the fore. The signs will be different for each of us, but are likely to include changes such as a rise in temperature, increased heartbeat and tensing of the muscles. Recognizing the signs that are the symptoms of the emotion is fundamental in identifying the emotion. More important is accepting such emotions as our own. This is a critical point in controlled demeanour, because any emotion, particularly anger, is the result of our own thought-processes. You may have heard people say things such as 'You made me angry' or 'She upset me': in a sense such statements are untrue. It is not possible for one person to control the emotions of another. Yes, he or she may do or say something which has an impact on our thinking, but our emotions come from our own thoughts and therefore it is the individual who is responsible for his or her own emotions. Having recognized our own role in developing our emotions and subsequently claiming them as our own is the first step towards managing personal anger.

There are a number of options as to how we deal with the emotion. There is no doubt though that finding some way of expelling our anger, or indeed managing it, is a much preferred option to storing it up. All the evidence suggests that storing up anger and hoping it will go away can turn into resentment and is likely to be expelled in an unmanaged way through, for instance, anger transference or long-term payback or other self-destructive acts.

If in a particular situation we have time available to expel our anger through other activity, this can be a cathartic experience. Some people do this through physical or other activity that is totally different from the anger-provoking situation. It is possible to channel one's energy, which may come from anger, into a constructive pursuit. For instance, if you are upset by a disappointment with one customer you might channel your energies into winning other customers.

History is littered with examples of people who have achieved great things through being driven by anger on a broader scale; take for example the case of Lee Iacocca who turned Chrysler around, driven by the anger he felt on having been fired from Ford. His sole motive was to beat Ford in the market-place and, for Chrysler, this was a very focused and constructive channelling of anger.

Another powerful approach to dealing with one's own anger is to use social support-systems. These could include family, friends and colleagues who provide support by allowing you to express your feelings. Often simply explaining your feelings to an independent person can help; he or she need not provide you with a solution or advice, just a 'shoulder to cry on'.

If we are in an anger-provoking situation which is spontaneous, then we may not have the time available for some of the activities mentioned above. In such circumstances, we need to rely on psychological techniques to manage emotion, and this means controlling our inner dialogues. Often the knee-jerk reaction when becoming angry is to generate negative inner dialogues. So, for example, we may say to ourselves: 'He really is being unreasonable. I heard that he was vindictive – this has confirmed it. He's out to get me. I'm going to show him – he won't get away with this. Just look at him, all smug and arrogant – that's just his problem. He needs someone to sort him out.'

Often such inner dialogues have little foundation in fact; they tend to be based on emotional and sometimes irrational reactions. We need to be aware of our inner dialogues and question whether they are well founded. Some people have described their capability to check and control inner dialogues; by turning the negative dialogues into positive ones they manage their own emotion more effectively. This technique, the APT technique, encourages us to become **aware** of negative inner dialogue, **pause**, and **thought select** a more appropriate dialogue. This seems to support the notion of some early religions that we should pray for our enemies. If able to do this, it becomes difficult to maintain our anger because the changed thinking changes the feeling.

The other psychological technique that can be effective is to put the anger-provoking situation into context. This means comparing it with other issues. For example, we could say, 'This really is not worth getting worked up about – there are more important things in life and this, after all, is only a work situation.' Equally, if we can put a situation into a time context, this can reduce the immediate stress; so we could say, 'Well, this may be a major problem right now, and currently I feel pretty angry, but I know that in a couple of weeks I'll be able to look back and laugh at the situation.'

Where you regularly experience difficulties of anxiety and anger, it is useful to write down all the things that you are currently worried or angry about and then to hide the list. After a week, return to it. You will probably be struck by how insignificant the issues that were causing you concern now appear. This sort of technique is useful for getting things into perspective.

MANAGING THE EMOTIONS OF OTHERS

Managing the anger of others is different from managing one's own anger. However, often the two matters have to be addressed at the same time. Frequently if someone else is angry and it is because of a personal confrontation with you, there is a distinct possibility that you too will become angry.

Managing the anger of the other person could mean simply allowing him or her to let off steam and vent anger. This may call for some strong self-discipline because allowing someone to show his or her emotion, particularly when it is directed at you, can be difficult.

When someone else is angry, the skills of active listening are particularly important. At a basic level, it means shutting up and letting the other person speak. At a more advanced level, it means showing empathy and understanding, which can be done without having to agree with the angry person's point of view.

It is important in the early stages to avoid being drawn into an argument. The fogging technique, which we discussed earlier, is a particularly useful way of diffusing some of the emotion. By agreeing in part with the other person's point of view, you provide him or her with what is wanted: attention. Furthermore you also show that his or her point of view is being listened to, even if you do not agree with the whole argument. Where others are involved, draw them into the conversation and remember always to stick to facts. Overall when dealing with the anger of other people, the most effective strategy is to remain controlled. In a sense, controlled demeanour is about remaining assertive in situations which could otherwise become very emotional. All the techniques of assertion are important, and there is a need to apply judgement in how and when they are applied.

OTHER BEHAVIOURAL **STYLES**

In this chapter we have discussed the philosophy of assertiveness as a behaviour, and looked at the practical steps and techniques of assertion. We believe that in most influencing situations it is preferable to adopt an assertive stance. There may, however, be some occasions when it is appropriate to adopt a more aggressive approach or indeed to take a passive position.

PAUSE FOR **THOUGHT**

Consider from your own experience situations of conflict where you have initially taken an aggressive approach.

1. *How does this compare with a passive approach?*
2. *How appropriate, on reflection, do you feel it was to take the approach you did?*
3. *In what circumstances do you feel it is appropriate to take an aggressive approach or a passive approach?*

In reflecting on the above questions, you may have identified that there are some situations when a more aggressive or passive approach is appropriate. If someone is using an overtly aggressive approach in order to intimidate you, then the only way to deal effectively with this is to challenge him or her. As previously described, in organizations there tend to be people who behave like the school bully; they take pleasure in putting down certain people, often easy targets. They may use one-line put downs such as 'What do you know?' or 'Who are you to comment?' Such aggressive approaches need to be met head-on and overtly challenged; this does not necessarily mean shouting and becoming emotional, but it could mean taking a stronger than assertive approach. It may also be appropriate to take a more aggressive stance if health or safety is at stake.

There may also be occasions when it is preferable to adopt a passive approach. One thinks particularly of situations where, for instance, you may want to gather more information, so that you can come back with a more assertive approach at a later date. Or you may decide to concede on an issue in order to provide psychological credits with another person. This creates a situation where the other person owes you a favour, which you may want to call in later on. In a negotiating context, a common convention is to make low-cost concessions in order to persuade the other person to give you something that you really want. In an influencing context, this could mean giving way on certain issues which you recognize to have less value, so that you can gain useful concessions from the other person.

To summarize, although we are advocating that the use of assertiveness is probably most appropriate in 80 per cent of cases, there will be other times when a more aggressive, passive, accommodating or avoiding approach is more suitable. This requires a high level of personal judgement. The real skill is in being able to make that judgement at the right time!

You have now covered each of the components of the Model of Successful Influencing. While reading this book you will have had ideas about things you now wish to stop, start or continue to do in order to enhance your abilities as an influencer. To translate the knowledge you have gained into real learning (you will recall the idea that real learning is not simply about knowledge or skills but about having the will to do something and actually doing it), we now encourage you to reflect upon the content of each chapter. We encourage you then to think about what you are going to do. To help you, we provide the next chapter, Into Action.

nine

INTO
ACTION

In the final chapter, we look at tools and techniques to help you implement and improve aspects of your influencing performance, and in particular we:

- explore the characteristics of readiness to undertake personal change;
- consider the use of learning logs as a way of capturing learning and improving performance;
- build on your understanding of how we can positively take control of inner dialogues and beliefs in order to enhance our influencing abilities;
- explain how to formulate your own self-assertion statements aimed at focusing on critical personal change;
- consider a powerful way of imprinting these new beliefs into our self-image, helping you build mental pictures and achieve your personal goals.

This chapter is very different from the others in the book. In it, we are going to look at ways of increasing the likelihood of you improving your performance as an influencer. The techniques we describe are both practical and psychological. Before we consider each of the tools, we ask you to look at the Model of Successful Influencing diagram, Figure 9.1, and recall and reflect on each of the skills of the influencing process. Once you have done this, we encourage you to look through the book, refreshing your memory, before identifying the issues and areas of influencing on which you want to focus. We will then ask you to consider some critical questions before deciding to change.

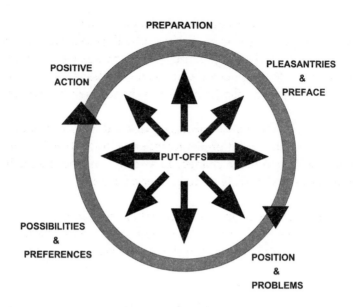

Figure 9.1 The Model of Successful Influencing

CRITICAL QUESTIONS BEFORE MAKING PERSONAL **CHANGE**

Listed below are some questions that our experience suggests need to be considered by the reader before trying to achieve personal change. Spend a few moments reflecting on these issues before putting together an action plan.

1. Do I really want this change?
Experience suggests that the most successful people are those who are strongly motivated towards achieving the change. Ask yourself how much you want it, and assess your answer on a scale of 0–10, where 10 is high. If your answer is less that 9, then your likelihood of success will be diminished. Are you truly open to the process? To what lengths are you prepared to go?

2. Am I prepared to take an active role in this process?
It is important to recognize that there is no such thing as instant success. In order to change, we need to not only be motivated but also be prepared to take an active role in the process. Are you ready to take these risks, and how will you deal with things if you stumble?

3. How will others respond to my change in behaviour?

If we initiate change in the way we behave, it will impact on other people. Ironically some individuals may prefer us to stay the way we are, as that way we remain predictable. If we change, it has implications for other people, and ultimately it may mean that they have to change their behaviour.

4. Will these changes cause me unnecessary discomfort or damage?

The golden rule for successful implementation is 'little steps for tiny feet'. This is about starting to make changes in a small way and gradually, after gaining some successes, moving on to greater changes.

5. Is this a good time to embark on making these changes?

You should reflect on whether this is the right time to make these changes. If many other things are happening at the same time, it may not be.

6. Who is available to help me?

Before embarking on the process of trying to improve your personal skills, you should think about who can help you or be of assistance. Such an individual need not be a subject 'expert', but should be somebody with whom you feel at ease. Ideally you should feel comfortable in discussing your action plans with him or her, and he or she should be prepared to continue reviewing your progress over some time.

7. What shall I do next?

The next step is to produce an action plan, which will act as your map as you try to bring about personal change. Our experience suggests that those individuals who are most successful in improving their performance do so primarily through the use of simple techniques. To help you in this endeavour, it is suggested that you compile a learning log as shown in Table 9.1.

USING LEARNING LOGS

Having reflected on the process and associated skills of influence and having answered the above questions, we now ask you to think about the things you want to stop, start and continue to do.

First, think about those aspects of your behaviour or the way you currently influence that you would like to **stop**, and list these in the first column of the learning log. Next, identify and list those things that you would like to **start**, which will improve your influencing skills. Finally, think about the way you influence and those things that you feel you do well. Record these in the **continue** column.

Try to have between five and nine items in each column; if you have many more, you decrease the likelihood of success. The log should be seen as a dynamic tool that will change over time, with items being either moved between columns or removed from the log while other things are added. It is suggested that for a minimum of three weeks you start each day by reviewing your learning log. Ideally the review should involve you in using your imagination and trying to visualize yourself with the desired outcome. This psychological process is now described in more detail.

IMPROVING THE PSYCHOLOGICAL CHANCES OF **SUCCESS**

In Chapter 3, we explored the concept of the self-image. Operating outside our self-image or comfort zone is a prerequisite for successful personal change. Traditionally in psychology, this has been achieved by one of two methods, flooding or desensitizing.

Flooding is the technique whereby we move a long way outside of our comfort zone and get 'flooded' with the experience. For example, a gentle

Table 9.1 Learning log

STOP	START	CONTINUE

person who believes that he or she is not particularly good at confronting others could be asked to represent the organization in a difficult confrontation with a trade union official known for his aggressive personal style. Most of us will have experienced this sort of approach, where it becomes a case of 'sink or swim'. Flooding is a common approach used in many organizations, and for many individuals it is a useful and expedient approach – they swim. Unfortunately, some people are not so lucky – they drown! Consequently, where this approach has been used unsuccessfully, the impact on the individual is not only highly stressful but can also be catastrophic: he or she may not try anything like it ever again.

Desensitizing is where the individual moves slowly, bit by bit, outside his or her self-image or comfort zone. This approach is often used in traditional training programmes. Typically on a training course we would increase the degree of complexity of role-plays as the learner becomes more proficient; in coaching, we are effectively shaping his or her behaviour. Desensitizing is more likely than flooding to ensure success, but it can take a considerable period of time, and still involves a level of applied risk-taking by the learner.

Both techniques are used frequently in clinical psychology to help individuals with specific fears or phobias; however, each is potentially damaging because of the need for the individual to change behaviour before having achieved the necessary internal changes. The result is always stressful for the individual.

More recently, studies by ourselves and others suggest that we can move outside our comfort zones primarily by managing our mental processes. In many ways this is akin to desensitizing, but takes considerably less time and is relatively stress-free. We shall be describing the use of self-assertion statements to achieve this. Where we find ourselves acting inconsistently with our self-image, then we are likely to engage in a range of psychological defence mechanisms, something which is discussed later in the chapter.

Let us now consider this model in action, using a storyboard to illustrate the key stages of the cycle. Some studies have shown that one of the things humans find most stressful is making a public presentation or speech. One recent survey revealed that public speaking featured at the top of a list of anxiety-provoking circumstances, while death was listed at number three. In other words, some people would rather die than make a presentation!

Storyboard: Overcoming a personal fear

Pauline was a successful administrator who was uncomfortable whenever she was asked to make a presentation or speech. She could trace her fear back to her childhood and an early experience in the classroom. On one occasion she had been asked to read in front of her class (**behaviour**) and because of perceptual distortions (seeing things incorrectly) and her accompanying negative inner dialogues, she believed that: other pupils were better speakers; she was being picked on by the teacher; and this task was a more important event than it really was.

Even before speaking, she had been heavily engaged in negative internal conversations (**inner dialogues**), saying things like:

- 'This is going to fail.'
- 'I had to read my poem before, and I was unprepared – it was a nightmare.'
- 'It will be so embarrassing.'
- 'The teacher (**"expert"**) is going to give me a bad report.'
- 'What will my parents (**"experts"**) say?'

Such negative inner dialogues indeed contributed to her physical manifestations (**behaviour**) such as perspiration, shaking hands, fast-beating heart (she thought others could hear it) and shuddering voice, and ultimately it was a rather less successful reading than it might have been. Overall the performance was not a total failure, but Pauline selectively noted the feedback of the more negative pupils in her class and again selectively recorded the negative aspects of the balanced evaluation from the teacher.

Over time, when similar situations were encountered, the same negative process was repeated, and as a result she developed a self-image that contained a negative belief about her ability to make presentations. (It is important to remember that this belief was based on her interpretation of events, rather than on reality.)

Later in her life, despite reaching a responsible position in business, she still held a profound fear of public speaking. By now this negative belief had become career-limiting.

The above illustration is about presentation skills, yet it is important to understand that it holds good for other beliefs, such as those indicated by the following statements:

■ 'I find it difficult to engage in small talk.'
■ 'I have never been comfortable when confronting others.'
■ 'I am naturally shy with others.'

An important issue to understand is that, in our storyboard example, Pauline does not necessarily have to conduct further presentations for the same negative and cumulative results to occur. This is because, simply by reflecting on the experience, the negative impact increases. In other words, the mental repetition is as powerful as the physical experience. If the experience is a particularly uncomfortable or painful one, then we are much more likely to engage in this process of repetition; and the process of repetition then imprints the image, which results in a reinforced belief.

What we are describing here is that in our minds, reality is often based on events that we have experienced in a very intense manner and, as a result of many mental repetitions, it becomes our truth. Hence the child who is frequently humiliated by his or her parents as being stupid or dim-witted feels the experience in a painful, acute way and, as a result of reflection, comes to believe what his parents say. This situation typifies that of many underachievers across many different spheres.

The other thing that is interesting in the above storyboard example is that it shows that, even when we have a belief that is self-limiting or restricting and, importantly, we are aware that it is, we still act in accordance with the negative belief. The reason is simple; we are acting in accordance with our self-image and beliefs about ourselves. We may not particularly like or enjoy our behaviour, but we are free from stress and anxiety because we are both predictable and consistent. These latter two characteristics are very important aspects of human behaviour. Let's consider how these beliefs develop using a storyboard example.

Storyboard: Developing beliefs

Carol Ann was flying from Los Angeles to Auckland via Honolulu. She was well travelled and flew thousands of business miles each year; she enjoyed the whole process of flying.

As the 747 gathered speed to take off from Honolulu, there was suddenly an enormous bang, which sounded like an explosion. All the passengers became aware that the aircraft was braking harshly and eventually it ground to a halt. Clearly the passengers were somewhat anxious. There were no announcements as to what had happened, but there was an air of chaos as they disembarked down the escape chutes.

Subsequently it transpired that almost at the point of take-off a front tyre had exploded. Although there was no imminent danger, the pilot had quite rightly pulled back from taking off. The aeroplane had come to rest about 200 metres from the end of the runway (and the sea).

Carol Ann returned to the terminal building with the other passengers. They were there for almost two hours and during that time they talked about their common experience. Every time they discussed the incident, Carol Ann found herself seeing it in her mind. In effect she was repeatedly imprinting the powerful experience.

She eventually arrived in New Zealand and once again she found herself recounting the story to different individuals. Each time she did this she continued to imprint the picture in her mind.

Although the incident happened only once, she probably thought about it several hundred (if not thousands of) times. As a result, her subconscious recorded it as if it had happened repeatedly. As a result of this repetition, Carol Ann developed a series of different beliefs about flying which included the following:

- 'Flying can be dangerous.'
- 'You have no chance if something goes wrong.'
- 'I don't like flying.'
- 'I get headaches when I fly.'

As a result, although she continued to travel extensively, she found that the experience was less and less enjoyable and more and more stressful. This was hardly surprising; when one of the authors met her, some eight years after the event, she was still able to recall the incident in vivid detail. In effect she was still imprinting the experience: it was still happening to her.

What the above story clearly illustrates is the ease with which we can develop beliefs based on intense real experiences that by repetition quickly become our reality. This is the way in which fears and phobias develop. We now want you to use your imagery skills to help you explore and develop the beliefs you hold about your influencing skills.

PAUSE FOR **THOUGHT**

Now let's consider the development of our imagery skills while at the same time improving our influencing skills.

Below you will read descriptions of seven general influencing situations, which include the key competences as described. This exercise will ask you to consider the situations and, by using as much imagery as you can, make the images as real as possible. We will then ask you to consider how effective your imagery skills are against four key criteria:

1. *How vivid was the picture image?*
2. *Were you able to hear sounds associated with the image?*
3. *Could you actually feel yourself doing something or taking action?*
4. *Were you able to experience any specific emotions associated with the image, for example being satisfied?*

Before you start these exercises it is important that you first try to relax fully. Ensure that you are sitting or lying down, make all your muscles go loose and try tightening each muscle in turn before relaxing. Take slow deep breaths and try to regulate your breathing. If necessary, start using positive inner dialogues to help you relax by silently repeating words or phrases like 'Be calm', 'Be still' or 'Peace'. It is only when you are relaxed that you are best able to practise your imagery skills.

In doing the exercises, try to see as much detail as possible; focus entirely on the image and prevent your thoughts from wandering. Visualize the following seven influencing situations. Spend at least a minute thinking about each of the situations. Think about what you are doing and how you are doing it. When imaging each situation, try to see, hear, smell or feel as much detail as possible.

1. You are preparing to influence someone whom you are meeting later that day.
2. You are in a situation where you are required to make a good first impression on another person.
3. You are quickly building a trusting relationship with another person.
4. You are showing powerful listening and questioning skills.
5. You are giving feedback to another person and it is being well received.
6. You are using strong persuasive techniques, including the use of appropriate body language.
7. You are in a situation where you are easily able to confront another person in an assertive manner, and you are able to control the way you respond when the other person becomes either manipulative or hostile.

When you have finished imagining each situation please rate your level of imagery skill using the following questionnaire, circling the response that best describes your level of achievement. Remember that, for the purpose of this exercise, 'image' is any sensory experience, whether seeing, hearing or feeling.

Self-assessment rating
1 = No image
2 = A fairly weak image
3 = A moderately clear image
4 = An extremely powerful image

Using the above rating scale, answer the following questions in respect of your imagined performance in each situation.

1. How clearly did you see yourself doing this activity?
2. Could you hear any sounds?
3. Could you feel yourself taking any specific actions?
4. How strong were your feelings?

Next think about the specific situation and the effectiveness of your performance in the context of using influencing skills. Use a scale of 0 (low) –10 (high).

1. How effectively did you feel you performed with the skill?
2. How could you improve your performance?
3. What could you do differently to make things more powerful?

Finally, repeat the process of using imagery in these seven situations. Keep repeating this process, and continue to assess yourself against the imagery rating, as well as assessing your perception of performance. In this way, you should be able to monitor your progress in improving your imagery and visualization skills, as well as in improving the competences of influencing.

SIGNIFICANT FEATURES OF OUR **RESEARCH**

In terms of thought processes and ability to visualize, there were some interesting patterns. High achievers tended to show the following significant similarities:

■ heightened awareness of the impact of other people, particularly negative impact, on their inner dialogues;
■ regularly engaging in the use of imagery, with an ability to experience actual feelings and see detail when fantasizing or using imagery;

■ frequently using 'internal coaching' to improve performance;

■ a tendency to encourage themselves either before, during or after doing something, particularly in threatening or potentially difficult situations;

■ recognition of the potential impact of negative thoughts and their own vulnerability if such thoughts are not managed;

■ the regular use of repetitive success-imagery to visualize how things might be in the future;

■ the ability to visualize big pictures, but with the capability of homing in on fine details.

APPLICATION IN PERSONAL CHANGE

Our findings are supported by some of the research into achievement of human potential in the sporting world, where it has been known for some time that mental practice and visualization can improve physical performance.

As long ago as 1965, experiments in examining methods of gymnastic coaching showed that it was possible for people to learn gymnastic skills simply by reading a mechanical analysis of the skills, combined with mentally practising (Jones, 1965). What was particularly interesting in these results was that this approach applied even when the learner had no previous experience of the skill.

Other more anecdotal examples include the recollections of the golfer Jack Nicklaus who in his book *Golf My Way* (1991) describes his use of imagery as follows:

> I never hit a shot, even in practice, without having a very sharp in-focus picture of it in my head. It's been like a colour movie. First I 'see' the ball where I want it to finish, nice and white and sitting up high on the bright green grass. Then the scene quickly changes and I 'see' the ball going there: its path, trajectory and shape, even its behaviour on landing. Then there's a sort of fade-out, and the next scene shows me making the kind of swing that will run the previous images into reality. Only at the end of the short, private, Hollywood spectacular do I select a club and set up the ball.

Similarly, in the clinical field, work with stutterers highlighted that stutterers held a stronger self-image of themselves as stutterers than as non-stutterers, and that because of this they felt more comfortable relating to the world as stutterers (Fransella, 1971). It was shown that with mental practice and visualization techniques the problem could be significantly alleviated.

In the medical context, there is a growing body of evidence to indicate the effectiveness of imagery in treating a spectrum of conditions ranging from depression to chronic pain (Schultz in Singer and Pope, 1979).

USING IMAGERY IN PRACTICE

We also asked those with strong powers of visualization whether their use of imagery is linked to any context or particular time of day. The majority said their strongest visualization experiences were when they were relaxed or semiconscious, being particularly vivid when in the state of limbo between wakefulness and sleeping in the morning or last thing at night. This is sometimes referred to as the 'alpha state': the body is relaxed but the mind is still working although with a slow-down in brain waves.

It is clearly possible consciously to harness these powers, and it appears that they are frequently used by high achievers (including sportsmen and women) and strong influencers. The primary technique to help us with mental readiness is that of self-assertion statements.

USING SELF-ASSERTION

Self-assertion statements are concerned with defining success as a goal. They are written in a specific way so that through the use of visualization, they can result in the goal being imprinted and becoming our new belief and ultimately, with repetition, our new reality. Self-assertion statements can be either temporary or permanent, and repetition can help us achieve lasting and sustained change in our behaviour.

Self-assertion statements are statements of desired outcomes or behaviours, which are written down and the associated images then imprinted on the mind. They accelerate the process of moving towards the achievement of personal goals and objectives by helping us imprint only the images we want into our subconscious, rather than other less beneficial messages.

Self-assertion statements are about establishing new beliefs and counteracting old ones about ourselves by effectively programming our subconscious. This programming is a normal and natural process; however, by using self-assertion statements we take control of the process, rather than leave things to chance.

Key steps in using self-assertion statements

The technique for using self-assertion statements follows three critical steps:

1. Identify and define the desired change, ie recognize what needs changing.
2. Draft self-assertion statements (making sure they subscribe to the principles described below) and ensure that they specify successful outcomes.
3. Imprint by reading the self-assertion statements at least twice a day, and use imagery to facilitate the resulting powerful changes in beliefs and subsequently behaviour.

How self-assertion statements work

They work by initially creating discomfort with our self-image, or how we see ourselves, and this discomfort increases the more we imprint the new images. Eventually, by repetition, we start to create a new dominant picture of reality as well as an increasing level of discomfort. Slowly we start to change our behaviour to match the new image or dominant picture of ourselves; then we begin to act in accordance with the new picture or belief.

Storyboard: Using self-assertion statements

Phil was concerned: he had a self-belief that he was not particularly willing to develop others in his team, compounded by a feeling that he was not very good at developing others. This belief would often show itself by his generally ignoring the signals when his subordinates gave signs that they needed his help.

After some time, this characteristic was picked up by his boss and Phil committed himself to doing something about it, but he knew it would not be easy, not least because he didn't really think he could do much actually to help his people.

Phil knew about the power of self-assertion statements. He already used them in improving aspects of his performance, so he decided to draft a new statement as follows: 'I am proud that every day I take time to help my people grow and develop.'

Each morning and each evening he read the statement and each time he tried to visualize a different image related to his helping develop his people. What he did not do was try to force himself to change his behaviour; he believed that if you changed the picture first, the behaviour would follow.

After a period of about 10 days, he became aware that he was doing something that gave him an opportunity to provide development for one

---

> of his staff. However, he did nothing and as a result of this he found himself feeling uncomfortable and engaging in various psychological defence mechanisms. His own favourite was rationalization: 'I would have helped him, but I have to get ready for the meeting tomorrow.'
>
> The more he read his self-assertion statement, the more his discomfort or stress seemed to increase. Consequently, after a period of about three weeks, Phil found himself unconsciously changing his behaviour to match his new picture of himself.

In the above example Phil changes his behaviour to escape from the stress he is experiencing by repeatedly reprogramming his self-image. The change is first made within him, and the behaviour follows. Phil will need to keep using the assertion statement for some time to ensure that what he has is a permanent change.

Developing powerful statements

There are a number of important principles for producing effective self-assertion statements, which, if adhered to, are likely to produce results.

1. Make them your own
You can only affirm for yourself. Do not try to affirm qualities or changes in other people or to correct or alter situations you cannot control. In writing your self-assertion statements, you are seeking to change your self-image, or how you see yourself. Only you can deliberately control the input of information and the visualization that brings about the change of your subconscious self-image. Therefore, in most cases, your self-assertion statements will start with the word 'I'.

As with most guidelines, there are exceptions. When you and another person have agreed on a joint goal, it is possible to write a 'we' affirmation. For example, you and your team could set an agreed joint goal; in this case you will need to affirm both the 'we' joint goal and your individual part of reaching the goal.

2. Particularly positive
Write out your self-assertion statements only in a positive way. Do not describe what you are trying to move away from or eliminate. You must vividly paint the picture of success for your subconscious in a positive statement. For example, do not make an affirmation like 'I am no longer poor at making social small talk', but make a positive statement like 'I make an immediate impact on people I meet', to enable you to picture the change you desire.

3. Only in present tense

Write out your self-assertion statements in the present tense. The reason we use only the present tense in describing our affirmations is that this is the only time frame in which the subconscious operates. Statements like 'some day', 'maybe' and 'tomorrow' will create pictures that make you feel detached from the behavioural change you want to experience now. You want to feel as though the change is already happening and that you are experiencing the change inside your own mind and body.

4. Avoid comparisons with others

The technique of self-asserting is a personal process. You are a unique person, and if you attempt to compare your behaviour with other people's, it will give you no personal way of measuring your growth progress. You may become discouraged by not measuring up to others, or you may get false clues as to the change in your self-image by being better than someone who is less capable. Do not affirm that you are as good as, or better than, anyone else. Just strive to bring about the changes in your self-image that you desire, by asserting the qualities that are best for you.

5. Paint the picture

Describe the activity you are asserting in terms that create pictures of you performing in an easy and anxiety-free manner. Your subconscious actions should be described by statements that start with 'I easily', 'I quickly', 'I enjoy', 'I love to', 'I thrive on' and 'I show'. Statements like these carry a picture of action and accomplishment that does not cause you to feel either threatened or pushed. The result is that you keep moving towards success with confidence.

Do not use just the ability 'I can' in your self-assertion statements because this will not produce change. You already have that ability. What you must indicate strongly is achievement. Statements like 'I am' and 'I have' express clearly to the subconscious the picture of the behavioural change you desire. In using self-assertion statements, you assume on the subconscious level that you are already acting like the person you want to become. The more you act subconsciously as if you are already in possession of that quality, the faster will your self-image make it evident in your daily actions. By seeing success, you also help eliminate some of the stress usually associated with trying to achieve a goal.

6. Particularly powerful words

Try to put as much power and excitement in the wording of your self-assertion statements as you can, by vividly stating your behaviour in colourful terms. Words that spark an emotional picture in your subconscious help to make the experience that is the subject of your assertion more believable and attractive. Write out your self-assertion statements in a manner that creates emotions such as fun, pride, happiness and accomplishment: the more emotion, the faster the change. Some examples of starting phrases include: 'I warmly', 'I happily', 'I lovingly' and 'I enthusiastically'.

7. Realize the achievable

It is important for you to assert only as much as you can honestly imagine yourself becoming or performing. The basic rule is not to overshoot or undershoot. Try to have such a clear and vivid picture of the end result you want to accomplish that you accurately stay on course with your goal.

In writing out your self-assertion statements, do not try to assert perfection. It is generally self-defeating to make assumptions about yourself or your accomplishments that you know have very little chance of ever happening or lasting. By using terms like 'I always', 'every time I', or 'I'll never' you can place unrealistic demands on your performance reality.

Clearly if you were to set a self-assertion statement of 'I enjoy the feeling of winning the London marathon', then simply reading the statement and waiting for the victory will lead to disappointment. It would be important to combine physical training with psychological technique. It is worth noting, though, that top athletes, who are often very close in terms of physical ability, will use psychological techniques such as self-affirmation statements and visualization to give them the physical edge over their competitors.

You should remember that your personal self-assertion statements should be for yourself only, because people may constantly try to remind you of the old self-image picture of yourself. Without really meaning to hold you back, the people around you may get upset when you start changing. If we reveal our personal goals and self-assertion statements to others, it allows them to work against us and very often causes us to fail to accomplish our goals. Use good judgement and only reveal your self-assertion statements to those people who need to know them and who can help you realize them more quickly.

Finally, a word of caution: we believe that the use of self-assertion statements is a powerful psychological tool that supports behavioural change by throwing your mental equilibrium into disorder. In view of this we suggest that when writing your statements you seek to write a number of different statements relating to various aspects of your life. These might include the following areas:

- health;
- job;
- family;
- leisure;
- finance.

Using this approach you are less likely to find yourself becoming so goal-orientated that everything else gets forgotten!

Some examples of self-assertion statements

There now follow four examples for each of four kinds of self-assertion statement, which you may find helpful. Some may fit your work situation, while others focus on improving aspects of your influencing skills. If some of these self-assertion statements fit your personal needs, please use them, but be sure to rewrite them if necessary so that they sound like you talking to yourself.

Management self-assertion statements:

1. I am an expert at delegating responsibilities and seeing our people experience the achievement of results.
2. I always find the satisfaction that comes from developing my people extremely rewarding.
3. I enjoy the results that come from positive thinking.
4. I consistently receive tremendous gratification from 100 per cent customer satisfaction.

Team self-assertion statements:

1. We treat each of our customers as though they are our only customer and the effect is that people come back to us, which really gives us a buzz.
2. We are truly professionals in our approach to all our job activities and we like the feeling of respect that this generates.
3. We pride ourselves on our company image in the community.
4. We easily keep our records up to date so that information can be quickly found.

Personal self-assertion statements:

1. I like and respect myself. I know I am a worthy, capable and valuable person.
2. I enjoy my life, my profession and my relationships with other people, and have a good balanced lifestyle.

3. I show others that I'm a person who does not give up easily.
4. I have had many successful experiences of using self-assertion statements and I take temporary setbacks easily.

Influencing self-assertion statements:

1. I am proud that I always make a positive impact on others, and that people warm quickly to me.
2. I am pleased that I am able to build relationships quickly.
3. I am grateful that I only confront other people using an assertive approach.
4. People always listen to me; my personal style is friendly and persuasive.

When you are satisfied with the wording of your self-assertion statements, transfer them to your diary, personal planner or personal computer so they will be easy to access. You may wish to make several copies; one to carry, one for your desk at work and another for the bedside. Organize them in any way you wish. Recognize that you'll be changing them frequently as you achieve existing goals and define new levels of success.

Imprinting your self-assertion statements

To imprint your goal on the subconscious requires the three-step process of reading, imaging and feeling.

1. Reading
Read the words of your self-assertion statements as many times as you can each day, thereby providing reinforcement. The best times to read and imprint are generally early in the morning soon after you wake, and just before you go to sleep. You can, however, read them at any time during your day, ideally when you are relaxed and have the available time. Repetition of the self-assertion statement is essential.

2. Imaging
As you read your self-assertion statements, you should be trying vividly to imagine or clearly to picture yourself having accomplished the change you want or the success you intend. You are displacing old self-images with new pictures of how you want to feel and act. Remember you are practising and experiencing the change consciously to begin with, but through your imaging you are recording the new images in your mind. Very quickly you will find yourself moving easily and naturally to the imagined levels of performance. Try to use visualization that helps you imagine sound, smells, the touch of something or how you feel.

3. Feeling

Feeling the emotion you want is very important for imprinting. Gather up the feelings you know will accompany the accomplished goal and enjoy them each time you imprint your self-assertion. The assertion will affect your system in a positive way in direct proportion to the extent to which you use vividness of imagery and emotional involvement.

Generally speaking, the impact in imprinting your affirmation can be measured as follows:

Just reading	10 per cent impact
Reading and picturing	55 per cent impact
Reading, picturing and feeling	100 per cent impact

PAUSE FOR **THOUGHT**

Consider your own goals. Try to identify at least two work-related, two personal and three influencing skills-related goals. Now follow the guidelines above for writing good-quality self-assertion statements.

1. *Practise the three steps of imprinting: reading, imaging and feelings.*
2. *Think about how you might be able to use self-assertion statements when working with others.*
3. *Practise drafting a team self-assertion statement.*

So far we have considered the use of self-assertion techniques of a permanent nature, that is to say those that are very useful in helping us challenge inappropriate beliefs held deep within us. They tend to require fairly extensive imprinting, and may need to be repeated over a considerable period of time. Nevertheless, if we are imprinting regularly, then usually we might expect to see some measure of improvement within about 21 days.

In using self-assertion statements, it is important to realize that you should not try to force a change in your behaviour. Keep reading the self-assertion statements, keep imprinting, but do not initially do anything different. If change is forced, then it will be similar to the 'white knuckle change' discussed earlier. The result of this is that we become stressed and are unlikely to continue with change. When the time is right, that is to say when you have reprogrammed your beliefs and established a new dominant picture of reality, then the necessary change will just happen naturally. What we are describing here is change that starts within us, and works its way out into our behaviour. This will be achieved without unnecessary stress.

Our research shows that while successful individuals use the kind of mental processes described in this book to achieve significant and lasting change to their self-image beliefs, they also use temporary self-assertion statements before particularly difficult situations.

A chief executive of an international petrochemical company described sitting down before a shareholders' meeting and using visualization to picture a successful result. This outcome included seeing and hearing the meeting clapping him, and seeing smiling faces.

Another executive from an international brewing organization stated that he would relax and use imagery before doing something demanding like informing people of major restructuring or redeployment. In such circumstances he recognized the picturing of a successful outcome as critical.

An international business professor explained that he had recognized the link between his thinking before starting an assignment and the eventual outcome. In particular he found that where he was able to visualize people wanting his help, or where he saw himself as being made welcome and quickly encouraged to contribute, then the outcome was infinitely more favourable. When he did not use such methods, the outcome tended to be less favourable. Consequently he developed a habit of using instant positive imagery on his way to the client's premises.

These sorts of techniques are similar to more permanent self-assertion statements. The primary difference is that they are not written down nor are they necessarily repeated. However, the principles of how they are developed still hold, ie they are first person, present tense, positive statements. Temporary self-assertion statements appear to be of particular value when there is little time to prepare. They are also useful in supporting more formal, permanent statements: it is in such a way that successful sports persons use the technique.

We can use these temporary self-assertion techniques when dealing with others. For example, when our associate consultants come to us with specific problems we might try this response, 'What would it look like if you didn't have this problem?' This sort of response forces the recipient to describe (and see) success. As discussed, this is the fundamental prerequisite and critical starting point necessary for achievement.

PAUSE FOR **THOUGHT**

1. *What is the best method of recording your self-assertion statements?*
2. *Are your self-assertion statements balanced across all aspects of your life?*

3. When or how would be the best time for you to imprint them into your subconscious?
4. How long are you prepared to use these statements to help you achieve lasting change?
5. In what circumstances would you feel that you could use a temporary self-assertion statement? Practise using this technique on something that you are going to do later on today.

We can draft self-assertion statements and, through imprinting, use them to change aspects of our own beliefs about ourselves that we have identified as self-limiting. Changing these beliefs will lead to more effective performance. Such techniques are ideal when dealing with significant or deep-seated beliefs about our self-image. In a similar way, we can use temporary assertions when we are suddenly faced with a difficult situation or one for which we have had little time to prepare or when we need to support a more formal self-assertion about a specific situation. We encourage you to use these approaches in order to bring about lasting change in your ability to influence others.

IN CONCLUSION

We have provided you with a framework, the Model of Successful Influencing, and used its stages to help you explore how you can enhance your understanding and abilities in this area. These ideas are not restricted to your working life; indeed we believe that the ideas presented and described will work effectively only if you use them holistically, that is in all spheres of your life. In this last chapter we have given you practical tools, including practical psychological tools, which you can use to help you put the ideas into practice. Whether you have read the whole book, or whether you have dipped in and out of it, we hope that you have found it helpful.

The authors are always pleased to hear from their readers either with specific questions about the subject matter or to provide general feedback, and can be contacted as follows:

Richard Hale
The Birches
2 The Dingle
Coombe Dingle
Bristol BS9 2PA
UK
Tel/fax: +44 117 968 2299

Peter Whitlam
Broom Hill
21 Cliff Drive
Cromer
Norfolk NR27 0AW
UK
Tel/fax: +44 1263 515150

REFERENCES

Back, K and Back, K with Bates, T (1982) *Assertiveness at Work*, McGraw-Hill, Maidenhead

Calvert, R *et al* (1980) *First Find Your Hilltop*, Century Hutchinson, London

Fransella, F (1971) *Personal Construct Psychotherapy and Stuttering*, Academic Press, San Diego, CA

Goleman, D (1996) *Emotional Intelligence: Why it can matter more than I.Q.*, Bloomsbury, London

Hale, R (1993) *How to Introduce Target Setting*, Kogan Page, London

Jessop, J (1994) *The Victorians*, Coombe Books, Surrey

Jones, J G (1965) Motor learning without demonstration of physical practice under two conditions of mental practice, *Research Quarterly*, 36, pp 270–76

Kolb, D (1984) *Experiential Learning*, Englewood Cliffs, New Jersey, Prentice Hall

Mehrabian, A (1971) *Silent Messages*, Wadsworth, Belmont, California

Nicklaus, J and Bowden, K (1991) *Golf My Way*, Reed Books, London

Pease, A (1984) *Body Language*, Sheldon Press, London

Schultz, D, Imagery and the control of depression, in (eds) Singer, J L and Pope, K S (1979) *The Power of Human Imagination*, Plenum, Dordrecht

Trompenaars, F (1993) *Riding the Waves of Culture*, Nicholas Brealey, London

Weyer, M V (September 1994) Mission improvable, *Management Today*, pp 66–68

Whetton, D and Cameron, K (1996) *Developing Management Skills for Europe*, Addison-Wesley Longman, Harlow

Wittig, A F and Belkin, G S (1990) *Introduction to Psychology*, McGraw-Hill, USA

FURTHER
READING

Barber, T X and Wilson, S C, Guided imaging and hypnosis. Theoretical
   and empirical overlap and convergence in a new creativity imagination
   scale, in (eds) Sheikh, A and Shaffer, T (1979) *The Potential of Fantasy
   and Imagination*, Random House UK, London
Buzan, T (1989) *Use Your Head*, BBC Books, London
Jaffe, D T and Bresler, D E, Guided imagery. Healing through the mind's
   eye, in (eds) Shorr-Sobel, J E and Connells, J A (1980) *Imagery: Its Many
   Dimensions and Applications*, Plenum, Dordrecht

INDEX

Visit Kogan Page on-line

Comprehensive information on
Kogan Page titles

Features include

- complete catalogue listings,
  including book reviews and
  descriptions

- on-line discounts on a variety
  of titles

- special monthly promotions

- information and discounts on
  NEW titles and BESTSELLING titles

- a secure shopping basket facility
  for on-line ordering

- infoZones, with links and
  information on specific areas of
  interest

PLUS everything you need to know
about KOGAN PAGE

http://www.kogan-page.co.uk